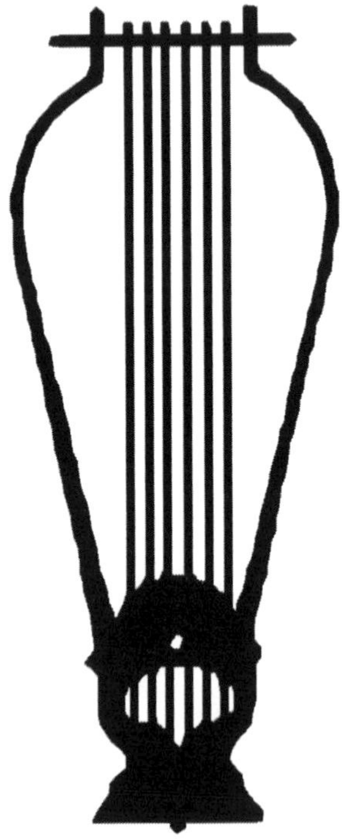

# TALES OF THE CURSE

## Feminine Secrets Unveiled

### by Peggy Lumpkin

This Edition
Copyright 2008 by Peggy Lumpkin
All Rights Reserved
Printed in U.S.A.
BookSurge Publishing
BISAC Category Women's Health
Library of Congress Catalog 98-73844
ISBN 1-4392-0348-2

This book may not be reproduced in whole
or in part, by electronic or any means
which exists or may yet be developed,
without permission of the author.

# Contents

**Part One**
**Tales of the Curse** 13
The Endless Highway 14
Barefoot Blunder 16
All Ears 18
The Pitiful Passenger 21
Red-Faced on the Green 24
All That Glitters 26
Conspiracy of Silence 28
The Absent-Minded Professor 30
Tampon Tantrum 31
Feline Fiend 33
Banking Blues 35
The Morning After 36
Shopping Snafu 38
Nowhere to Hide 40
Poppies in Bloom 42
Fly Your Flag 45
Finish Line 47
Trick or Treat 48
Short Shorts 49
I Must Leave the Country Now 50
Naughty Bits 51
Pinch Hitting 53

**Part Two**
**The Men in Menstruation** 55
God Must Be a Guy 57
House of Estrogen 59

From the Mouths of Babes   61
Interiors by Junior   64
It's a Bird, It's a Plane, It's Midol Man   67
Sweet Bird of Youth   68
Beloved Wimp   70
A Gallant Geek   72
Poker Faces   75
Having a Blast   77
A Cop Stopper   78
Excuse Me!   80
For the Man Who Has Everything   82
The Unflappable Gourmet   85
The Punching Bag   87
My Monthly Monster Man   89
Dad of the Year   91

**Part Three**
**Welcome to the Club**   93
Urgent News   94
Little Miss Literal   97
Playing Hooky   98
What's For Lunch?   100
Double Trouble   103
Tampon Taboo   105
Puppy Love   108
Two Rites of Passage   111
On Your Toes   112
Motel Hell   114
Spotlight and Stage Fright   117
Why White?   119
Dilatation and Curettage   120
Grace Period   122

Only in Hindsight   122
Too Frugal   123
Sink or Swim   125
My Shadow   127
Cheerleaders   128

**Part Four**
**The Crone Zone**   131
Coming into Heat   132
Surf's Up   134
Groovin' Grandma   136
New-Fangled Contraptions   139
Achtung, Herr Doktor!   140
Seiri-yo No   142
Old Dog, New Trick   145
The Mother of All Excuses   146
Old Faithful   149

**Part Five**
**Feeling No Pain**   151
A Little Magic   153
Many Moons   153
All New and Improved   155
Is It Terminal?   157
Pins and Needles   159
Rags Revisited   161
My First Moon   163
Red Cross and Leeches   165
PMS No More   167
Party On   169
Daughters of Eve   171
Nature's Way   173

Cosmic Cramps   174
A Rose Is a Rose   178

**Part Six**
**The Power and the Punishment**   179
Magical Menstrual Tour   181
Oriental Ovulation   183
The Western Womb   185
African Attitude   186
PMS, Pretty Mean Stuff   188
Menstruating Men   190
Moon Lodge Mysteries   193
The Red Tent   196
Maidens and Mothers   199
Fruit of the Womb   202
The Great Secret   205
The End of Innocence   206
An Act of Congress   209

**Part Seven**
**Ebb and Flow**   211
A Young Voice Still Speaks   213
Wise Wound   214
Glow with the Flow   217
The Teen Scene   218
All Together Now — 1,2,3   221
The Body Keeps Score   222
The Genius Uterus   225
Thoughts R Us   228
Lady Wisdom   231
Ancient Future   232
She Had Many, Many Names   233

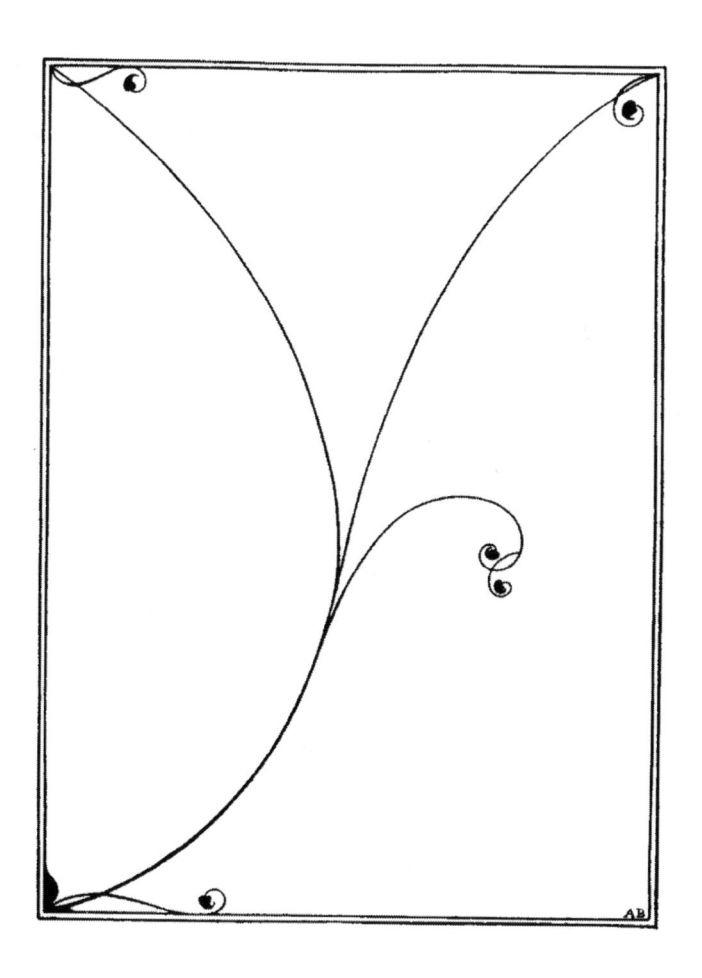

# Author's Note

This strange little book chose me as the person to put it down on paper, and I didn't understand why until it was almost finished with me. At first, I thought it was so that I could share some great laughs about a taboo subject, but then I began to realize that I was learning something in the process. The idea for this book came after I listened in hysterics as a group of friends unloaded a fantastic batch of stories about personal experiences with their menstrual cycles. I cringed and howled until I cried, listening to seemingly unbearable stories of humiliation, pain, and panic. Thinking there must be other entertaining anecdotes out there, I started collecting more stories through questionnaires, interviews, and e-mails. What I didn't realize was that these stories would forever change the way I look at my body. Some of the personal stories I received, as well as anthropological studies I uncovered, told of menstrual practices that made me shudder. Fascinating as they were, I did not include the more gory or explicit details that would offend mainstream sensitivities. I wanted this book to be heart-warming, not blood-curdling.

When you read the stories in the first section, *Tales of the Curse*, from women whose unpredictable uteruses put them in memorable plights, you will laugh and feel compassion. Gradually, a picture will begin to form about why the women in our culture suffer so much with their periods, why they tend to view them negatively, and why it is such a taboo subject. In *The Men in Menstruation*, you will read of the men, from youths to seniors, who thwarted or supported the menstruating women in their lives. *Welcome to the Club* will be familiar to every woman, with its stories of menarche, the onset of menses, and the traumas of the first tampon. We hear from the wise ones, in *The Crone Zone*, stories told by women whose uterus may have retired long ago, but whose memories are forever young. In *Feeling No Pain*, we listen to women who seem to have a new attitude about their body and its cycles, but who actually have taken a psychological step back toward the ancient ways. *The Power and the Punishment* looks at menstrual superstitions and attitudes around the world and how they are changing. Then in *Ebb and Flow*, we hear healing words from doctors, sociologists, and clergy. You will discover that there is a way to better women's health, but it's not in a pharmacy.

   The ancient tradition of women's circles is still intact. Though we may no longer gather in a menstrual hut or sit around a village fire, today we can find our women's circle on talk shows or in chat rooms on the Internet. This book, too, is a women's circle, where women regale you with intimate memories from the depths of their souls. Here you find a snapshot of the feminine mystique, warts and all, at the beginning of the new millennium.

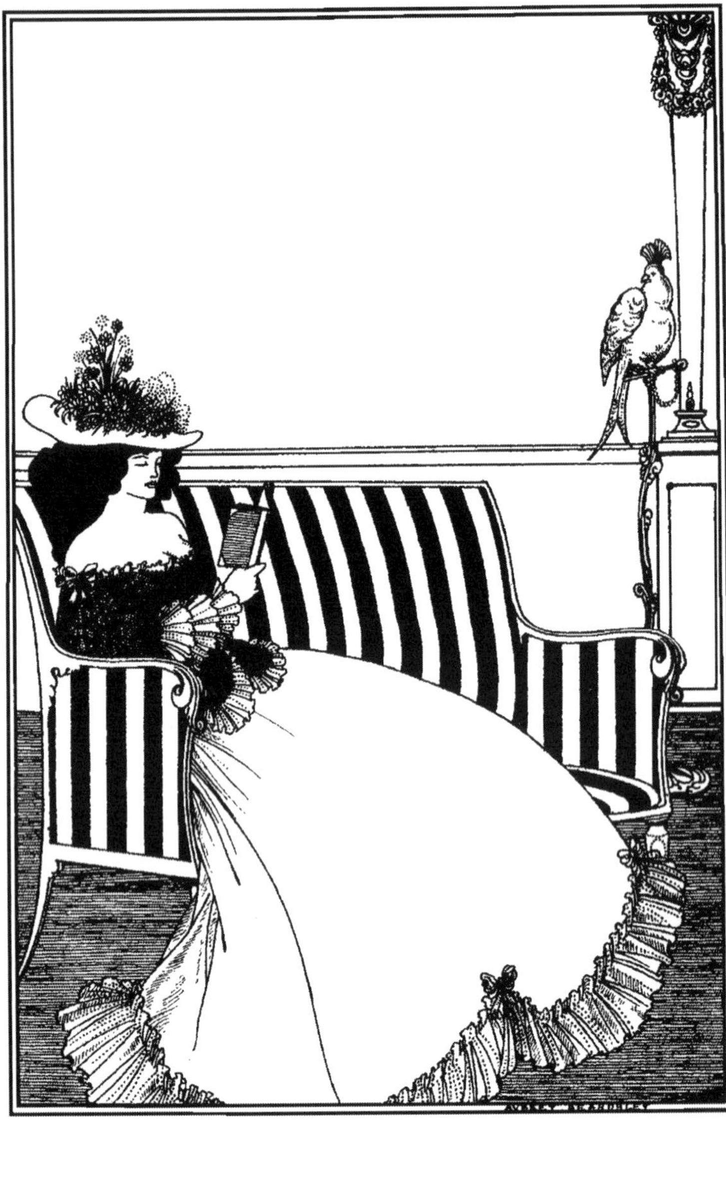

# Part One

# Tales of the Curse

As you read of the predicaments that are firmly etched into the memories of these women as they recall unforgettable episodes, you may snicker. Occasionally, a tear may threaten when one of the stories strikes home and you remember being affected by your own experiences. Each person was simply asked to tell a memory related to the menstrual cycle and was assured anonymity. Our contributors range in age from sixteen to ninety-two and have lifestyles that vary from nun to dominatrix, from welfare recipient to the wealthy. Despite the women's diverse lives and experiences, they all share a common ride on Mother Nature's roller coaster, and they all speak from their hearts. These are the memorable stories of the menstrual accidents that made them want to be swallowed up by the earth at the time, but now bring a smile.

The illustrations in this book are the work of the late nineteenth-century artist Aubrey Beardsley. Today's woman may feel she is measured against Playboy Playmates or Victoria's Secret models, but the nineteenth-century woman had to compare herself with Beardsley's beautiful, but equally idealized female images. So as you read these modern stories, the contrast of the century-old illustrations will serve as a constant reminder of our inheritance of Victorian morality, from which we are still slowly emerging.

# The Endless Highway

"My parents must be closet masochists. Why else would they have voluntarily tortured themselves by packing up the kids every summer and taking us on a vacation in the car? We would always start out with a AAA map that had ink marks on the places where we would stop each night. Dad's major objective was to drive us from ink mark to ink mark each day. Getting three kids rousted and organized each morning was a marathon of lost socks and sibling squabbles, all in the name of fun. The one cardinal rule of the road was 'Go before you get in the car.' Two kids would sit in the backseat, and we were rotated for the privilege of sitting between Mom and Dad on the bench seat in the front of the Chrysler. The two kids in the backseat had an imaginary line of demarcation separating their territories. Crossing that line invariably prompted tattling 'Mom, he's on my side!' or 'Mom, she's touching me!' These complaints were interlaced with singing countless rounds of 'Ninety-nine bottles of beer on the wall, ninety-nine bottles of beer,' and asking 'Are we there yet?' Mom was the designated dispenser of justice while Dad concentrated on covering distance. As hours passed by, Dad's knuckles would get whiter and whiter on the steering wheel.

"It was in this context that I found myself in the backseat at age twelve, on the way to Mount Rushmore, when I realized that I had started my period. I told Dad I needed to stop, and of course he immediately asked why I didn't go before I got in the car. I was informed that we had two and a half more hours to drive before stopping. I kept on telling him that I really needed to go, and Dad kept telling me that I should have thought of that before we left and that I would just have to wait. I could not bring myself to tell him the real reason in front of my two younger brothers. I kept hoping Mom would turn around and look at me, so I could signal toward my crotch to let her know what the problem was. But, as the designated navigator, she was too busy trying to find our next turn on the map and refereeing my brothers' burping contest at the same time.

"Finally, I gave up and resigned myself to just sitting there as I felt the puddle underneath me growing. When, after several wrong turns, we made it to our destination for the day, I waited until everyone else was out of the car and assessed the stain on the car seat. I pulled my shirttails out to cover my rear and went to tell Mom, who in turn cornered Dad. Apparently Mom deftly boomeranged the fault onto Dad's shoulders because I heard her saying, 'This wouldn't have happened, Frank, if you would just take a few minutes to stop, for heaven's sake.' Dad retreated with a bottle of Schlitz.

"I got to sit in the front seat the next day, and I'm certain that residents in the next state must have heard my brothers arguing about who had to sit on the stained back seat. From then on, I had absolutely no trouble getting Dad to stop the car for me whenever I wanted. In fact, he would even say, 'There's a gas station coming up. Do you need to stop, Honey?' This earned me the reputation with my little mongrel brothers as being Daddy's pet. But that didn't matter because, from then on, I was in the real driver's seat."

*Tales of the Curse*

# Barefoot Blunder

"Shoe shopping at my favorite department store used to be just about my most cherished thing to do. Nothing makes you feel as pampered as having someone kneel to wait on you. And seeing that unscarred pair of new shoes emerge from the crisp clean tissue in the shoebox was always like a rebirth for me — like opening a fresh bar of soap or a new box of crayons. But these days, I mail-order shoes from catalogues because one poorly timed shopping episode ruined the experience for me forever.

"That day, I had dressed in a fairly short skirt because I needed to try on boots and didn't want to bother with hiking up a long skirt or slacks. The sales clerk was an adorable young man who cheerfully appeared with a huge stack of boxes with all of the styles and colors of boots I had pointed out to him on our tour of the displays. As the salesman patiently helped me try on boot after boot, I realized to my horror that my period had started. Once she gets that signal from her henchmen hormones, my uterus has the habit of flooding as though a plug has been pulled from a dam.

"I could tell I had saturated the beige upholstered chair I was sitting on. I didn't want to stand up to try on any more boots, nor did I want to confess my dilemma to the salesman. So I told him that I liked the last pair of boots I had tried, but they felt too tight. Could he please check and see if they were available in a half size larger? As soon as he was out of sight, I pawed through the mountain of open boxes and boots to search for my own shoes. They had ankle straps, but I didn't want to risk taking time to buckle them (even though you can cook a pot roast faster than some clerks can find a shoe size in the back room). I just grabbed my purse and hobbled out of the store as fast as my flopping shoes would allow.

"To this day, I have never returned to that shoe department, even though the salesman is probably no longer there. I don't feel so badly about the prosperous store's ruined chair, but it still bothers me that I took so much of that patient salesman's day, and he didn't earn a penny's commission."

# All Ears

"As my books and motivational lectures grew in popularity, I began speaking to larger and larger audiences. Since I like to move around the stage and go into the aisles to interact with people, I purchased a cordless microphone.

"I love to wear white onstage because I feel it gives a friendly impression, and this particular day was no different. I wore a tailored white coatdress trimmed with gold buttons. I started my speech from the podium and, as I looked around the large audience of insurance executives, I felt my opening gambit had heightened their interest. My euphoria quickly evaporated, however, as I felt that telltale rush of liquid warmth between my thighs, heralding my red-calendar day. I had goofed. Trying to stay cool, I announced to the audience as graciously as I could that we would be taking a five-minute break, before jumping into the 'meat' of the presentation. With my knees locked together, I toddled off the stage and found the conference coordinator hovering just behind the big doors in the hall.

"I hissed through clenched teeth, my eyes flashing an S.O.S., 'Quick, which way to the closest ladies room? Can you believe my luck? I just started my period.' With a sympathetic nod, the young woman took my arm and hurried me off in the direction of the women's sanctuary, which, unfortunately, was located at the opposite end of the convention hall.

"I begged her to hurry before I bled through my dress. 'I'm so embarrassed. Here I am in front of hundreds of people, and blood is running down my legs. Oh, my God! I hope nobody noticed. What a mess.' I babbled on and on.

"When we got to the bathroom, we realized that neither she nor I had brought a purse and therefore had no change for the tampon machine. I pounded noisily on the metal box, throwing in a few choice words, hoping it would release a tampon. Just then, a lady emerged from one of the stalls, and I asked her if she could lend me change for the dispenser. She had no change, but after burrowing through her purse — the size of a feedbag — she triumphantly handed me a dog-eared tampon that had probably been sitting at the bottom of her handbag since World War II.

"Profuse words of gratitude rolled out of my mouth, as I babbled on like a windup toy about my white dress, my legs, my audience, my mortification. My benefactress just laughed and said, 'Get a big purse and carry a spare!'

"Once again tidy and secure, I strode confidently back into the conference hall to continue where I had left off.

"Usually it takes several minutes to pull a group back together from a break and get their attention focused again. But when I returned to the podium, people were sitting in their seats, surprisingly quiet. I reached up to the left lapel of my dress to turn on the microphone. I froze. This time my blood rose to my face, and I must have glowed like a neon sign. *My cordless mike had been on the whole time,* and it had faithfully relayed to my distinguished audience my babbling, my expletives, my menstrual history, and the Niagara Falls thunder of the flushing toilet. A quick death sounded inviting at that moment. What to do? What to do?

"I believe there is no such thing as an accident and that each of us encounters defining moments in our lives. Shakespeare wrote, 'There is a tide in the affairs of men which, taken at the flood, leads on to fortune. Omitted, all the voyage of their life is bound in shallows and in miseries.' Shakespeare probably wasn't talking about my precise situation, but I decided to jump right into the flood with both feet.

"I took a deep breath, looked into the upturned faces of my audience and, as a huge smile spread across my flushed face, I said, 'Well, now that you've gotten to know me a whole lot better, let's continue.'

"For a moment, a soft chuckle hovered over the room like a friendly cloud. Everyone relaxed and looked relieved. I realized something important that day. The audience was nervous when I came back because they were worried that I would freak out when I realized my horrendous blunder. As soon as I signaled to them that I was all right, I felt the energy in the room change. The big lesson I learned was how extensively our emotions affect other people. And of course the other lesson was, whenever you go to the bathroom, be sure to turn off your microphone."

# The Pitiful Passenger

"In high school, the school nurse got used to seeing me like clockwork every month, because I always vomited on the first day of my period. Besides terrible cramps, I would have a slight fever and diarrhea. My doctor, a man of course back in those days, told me it was simply dysmenorrhea and that I would have to learn to live with it. He gave me a barbiturate pain prescription that made me even more nauseated because he forgot to mention to take it with lots of water. Luckily, the school nurse was more sympathetic because she went through the same torture as I did. She provided me with a sanctuary month after month, through all my years of high school.

"When I started attending a big university, I had an hour bus ride to and from home every day, so on the first day of my periods, I stayed home until the worst hours were past. Unfortunately, one day I got to school and my period started in the afternoon. I didn't know where to take refuge and couldn't imagine there would be a sickroom nurse anywhere on campus. I decided to catch the first bus for home and hoped I'd make it to the safety of my house before the hormones pulled out the big artillery.

"The bus was packed, but I managed to find a seat toward the back. The diesel fumes were no antidote for nausea. I kept telling myself I could hold back my rebelling stomach by breathing deeply and thinking about something pleasant. But one pothole too many sent me running down the aisle of the bus. As soon as I said the word 'sick,' the bus driver pulled over to the curb for an unscheduled stop. I had grabbed my bags, thinking he wouldn't be able to wait for me. But as I stood on the sidewalk, barfing into the gutter, I realized that, not only was he waiting for me, but I had an audience of curious bus riders as well.

"When the retching subsided, I climbed back on the bus, thanked the driver for waiting, and took the longest walk of my life to the back of the bus. I avoided eye contact with anyone, including the tittering boys who obviously thought seeing a person puke was a stroke of great fortune. The bus traveled in slow motion in the stop-and-go traffic, and I was certain the trip would never end.

"I was all right for a little while, but sure enough, the nausea reared its ugly head and forced me to the front of the bus again. I must have looked pretty pitiful to the bus driver when I assured him it was all right if he went on. But again, as I vomited the final contents of my stomach, he patiently waited for me to come back on board. This time, a kind woman offered me her seat in the front row, where I sat with my forehead resting on the cool chrome handrail. At each stop, the exiting passengers would look to see what kind of shape I was in, but I just kept staring at the floor. I eventually made it to my bus stop, and with a final spray of fumes in my face, the bus took off while people watched me from the back window.

"Later, my younger sister told me that her best friend had been on that bus and saw the whole show. She overheard other passengers discussing whether or not I was a wino, and she had never felt so sorry for anyone in her life. I made it a point after that to explore the campus, where I found the infirmary with a sympathetic nurse who let me vomit in peace every month."

# Red-Faced on the Green

"Every year I volunteer as a scorekeeper for the LPGA. As a golf enthusiast, you can imagine how excited I was to get the chance to keep score for Nancy Lopez and Amy Alcott. As two of the most popular lady golfers on the tour, they normally attract a following of 300 to 400 spectators as they play. Well into their round, I got those signals from 'south of the border' that told me I had started my period. As soon as we got close to a bathroom on the golf course, I ran between holes and found the only available supplies — pads with wings. Realizing I had already soaked my underwear, which could in turn stain my white walking shorts, I decided to improvise and use the pad upside down on the outside of my underwear, thinking at least my outer shorts would be safe.

"As the game wore on, I realized the wings that were anchoring the pad to my underwear were chafing the daylights out of my thighs. But the scorekeeper's job is crucial in golf competition, and I was determined to finish. As we reached a par-3 hole, it dawned on me that the wings were no longer uncomfortable. In fact, it felt as though they were no longer there. In panic, I lower my clipboard in front of my crotch, so I could discreetly poke around for the pad, which was not an easy task with an audience of several hundred, all of whom I was certain were watching me. I could not find any trace of the pad, so I just froze in my tracks. Using my peripheral vision, I surreptitiously glanced around the area, only to have my worst fears confirmed. My face probably went purple as I watched the marshal gingerly carry my winged pad with his fingertips to the closest waste can. He called for silence as the golfers prepared to tee off and then washed his hands in green Gatorade, apparently the only liquid available. I prefer to never know whether anyone realized the pad was mine. This was definitely a case where ignorance was bliss. I made it through the entire round, and as memorable as it may have been for me, I couldn't even tell you who won."

*Tales of the Curse*

# All That Glitters

"Mornings are always hectic around our house as I struggle to get the kids ready and out the door in time for the school bus. One morning, my son, who always puts things off until the last minute, was frantically trying to finish up an art project due at school that day. The breakfast table was strewn with construction paper, scissors, glue, and a bottle of glitter. By the time he finished his masterpiece, it was too late to catch the school bus, so I told him to clean up his mess while I ran to throw on a jogging suit. (I've learned the hard way that it's best not to drive your kids to school in your nightgown thinking you won't see anyone you know.)

"By the time I got back home, I realized I didn't have time to shower and dress and still be on time for the appointment for my annual Pap smear and pelvic exam. So I grabbed a washcloth sitting on the bathroom counter and quickly gave myself a sponge bath, swiping 'hither and yon,' as my mother used to say. I sped off to my doctor's office and soon found myself in that unique position that makes every woman cringe — flat on my back, feet in metal stirrups, and a bright light illuminating my lower unit. As my gynecologist began his probing, he said 'Well, I see you really went all out for this exam.'

"I had no idea what he meant, but my mind started coming up with the worse possible scenarios, driven by guilt about not taking time for adequate hygiene. When I got home, I marched straight to the bathroom to take a proper shower. As I was taking off my top, I noticed a sparkle of light reflecting in the mirror from under my arm. I lifted my arm to inspect my armpit and was surprised to see multi-colored glitter. The light slowly dawned, and I picked up the washcloth I had used earlier. It was covered with the spilled glitter that my son had cleaned up from the kitchen table. I had been in such a hurry to tidy myself that I hadn't realized I was transferring the glitter to all regions. No wonder my gynecologist had been impressed! He probably doesn't see much decoration in his work."

# Conspiracy of Silence

"When I was just starting out in real estate sales, I had the fortune of falling into negotiations for a home that could truly be called a mansion. I was in way over my head, but I figured, 'What the heck. How else are you going to learn?' I had to present an offer to the owners of the home and wanted desperately to not look like the rookie I was. Dressed in white slacks, I rang at the front door and was greeted by the elegant lady of the house. She showed me to her gorgeous living room where her husband had me sit on a white sofa as he grilled me and tried to get me to reduce my commission. I was nervous and sweaty, but was holding my own, until I realized I had started my period. As the negotiations dragged on, I tried not to think about what was underneath me. I could tell I had bled all over the slacks and the sofa, but I just couldn't look down. When we finally reached an agreement, I made my way out of the house without turning away from the couple. At the front door, I backed my way to my car as they said good-bye.

"The next day, I had to go back to their house for counter-signatures. I decided I would insist on replacing their sofa. I was sure my commission would more than cover it. So I went back to their home, dressed in black and fully protected with a tampon, plus a super-size Kotex for extra insurance. This time they showed me to their study, where we signed the papers without comment. I debated whether I should voluntarily bring up the subject, or whether it would be too embarrassing for them. In the end, I said nothing. Sometimes, silence is golden."

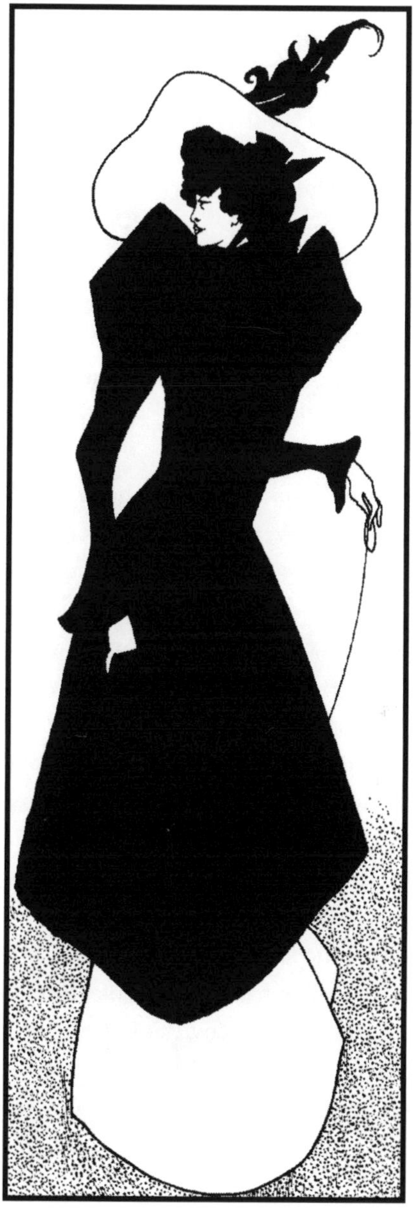

# The Absent-Minded Professor

"The first time my mother told me a grown up joke, I have to admit, it was not particularly funny. But I was thrilled that she considered me mature enough to hear it. Here's the joke. A secretary sat busily typing away, with a Tampax over one ear. Someone walked up to her and said, 'Hey, why do you have a Tampax over your ear?' The secretary pulls the Tampax out from her ear, looks at it (Mom's pretending she's the secretary as she tells it) and says, 'Hmmm. I wonder what I did with my pencil!'

"The joke is stupid because nobody could ever be that absentminded. Right? Well, maybe she could. As an underpaid and overworked professor in a small college, I tended to have a dozen things on my mind at once and never wanted to waste a minute. So when I started having a strange vaginal discharge that persisted several weeks, I muscled my way into an appointment with the physician who visited the school infirmary. 'How long since your last period?' the doctor asked as I lay with my feet in those wonderful stirrups. 'Oh, about a month or so,' I said. I couldn't be bothered keeping track of such things, although I knew I usually had about a 35 day cycle. 'Well, I would recommend you remove your last tampon when you're done from now on,' he said as he pulled out the remnants of a tampon that had spent a month smoldering and fermenting inside me. Why I never got toxic shock syndrome I'll never know. I considered it a cheap lesson, albeit embarrassing, about paying better attention to my body."

# Tampon Tantrum

"There is nothing worse than skiing in ill-fitting ski boots. No matter how much pain you're in, when you're at the top of a run, you have no choice but to ski down. Consequently, I spent a small fortune replacing my old vise-grip boots with a pair of state-of-the-art, high-tech wonder boots. They were custom molded with the aid of a computer to fit my feet perfectly. The boots had shiny fittings and neon graphics that looked like something from an outer space movie. The money I spent on them could have fed a family of three for half a year. I was so excited to try them out and then horrified when the left boot started hurting almost immediately. It felt very tight and lumpy.

"After the first run, my left foot went numb and I had to stop skiing. Irate, I stomped back into the ski shop and demanded a refund, custom fit or not. I was not polite to the poor salesperson when he asked me to sit down and let him see if he could figure out why the one boot was so painful. He stuck his hand down inside the boot and said, 'There seems to be something inside here.' When he pulled out his hand, he was holding a tampon. My jaw dropped. I apologized profusely. I must have put a spare tampon into one of the many pouches and pockets on my ski parka, but somehow the offending object had fallen into my boot. Normally, I wouldn't have been such a cranky customer, but there is nothing worse than sore feet.

"My advice to skiers: always check out your equipment thoroughly before you head up to the slopes. Make sure your bindings are tight, your goggles are clear, and your boots are free of sanitary supplies."

*Tales of the Curse*

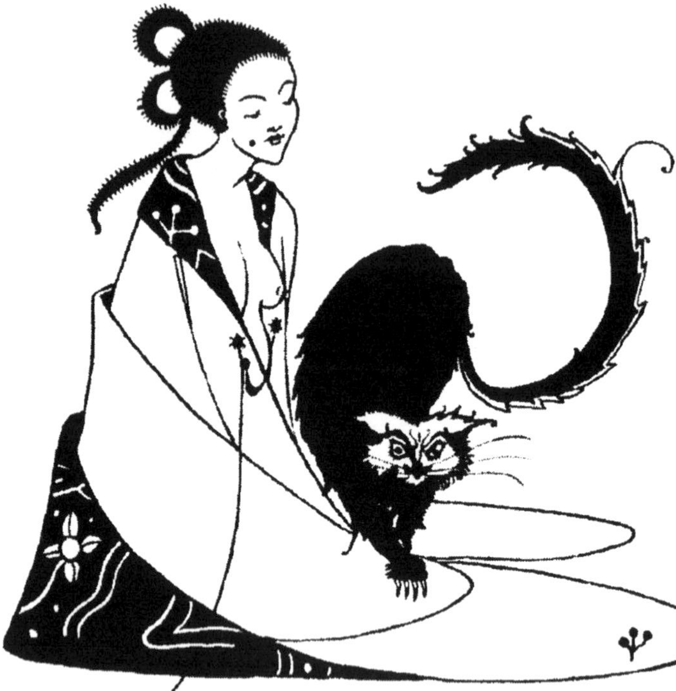

# Feline Fiend

"To have a boy come to your home to pick you up and publicly declare that he likes your company is a special event in any girl's life. At fifteen, I hoped dating would be more fun than that other rite of passage I had already experienced: menstruation. The night of my first date, I was nervous because my parents were skeptical about my dating. When my boyfriend arrived, I introduced him to my parents with the formality of an ambassador inveigling foreign aid. We were trying to find common ground and make some idle chatter when the family cat pranced into the living room, proudly displaying her catch — a heavily soiled Kotex.

"Dad tried to minimize everyone's embarrassment by leaping at the cat to get her out of the room. But Kitty just thought a fun new game was afoot as she ran around the living room. She thought the roles were reversed from all those times Dad had teased her with cat toys held just out of her reach. I guess she liked seeing Dad pawing at her new toy. Mom finally told my red-faced date and me to go ahead. 'It was a pleasure meeting you,' he lied as we left Dad trying in vain to appeal to the cat's non-existent sense of compassion.

"When my friend had the nerve to ask me out on a second date, my parents viewed him with a fair amount of respect, for stepping up to the plate again after that first date debacle. But from then on, Kitty remained safely locked in the laundry room on date nights."

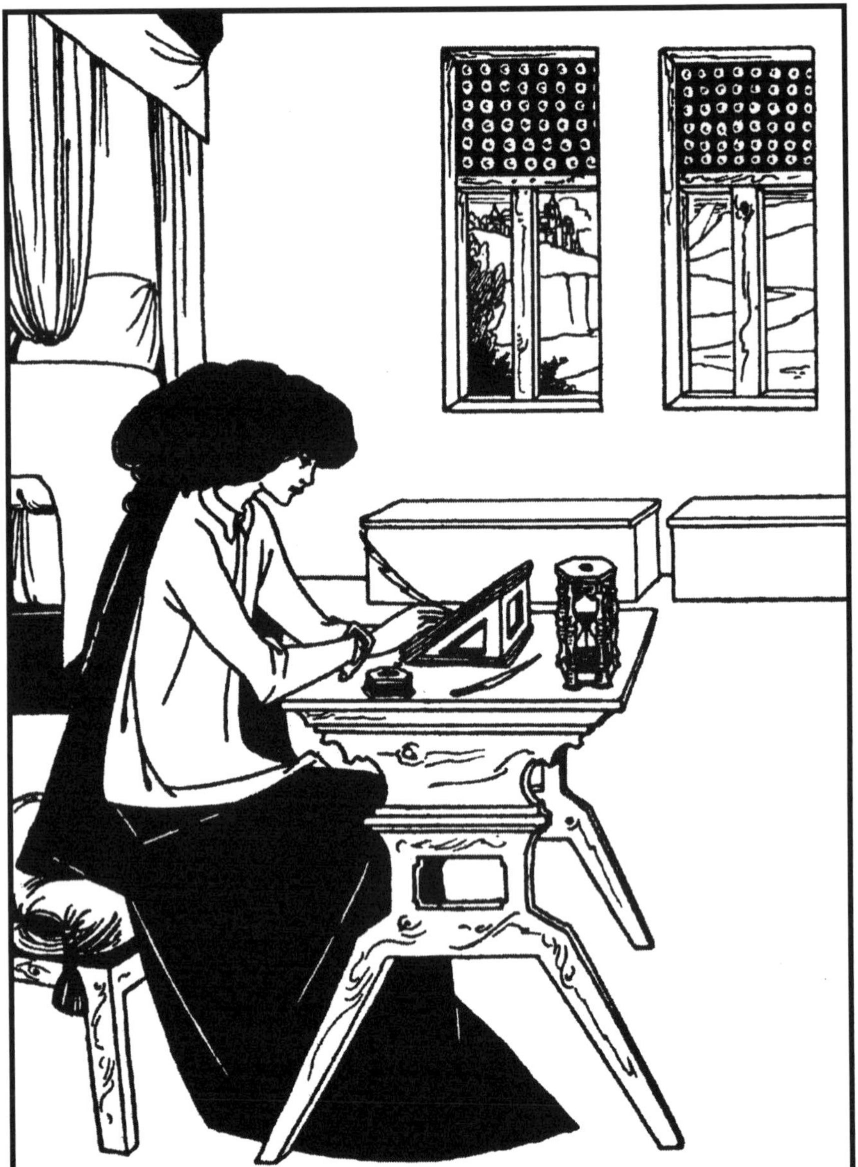

# Banking Blues

"I had always made my living as a waitress in my teens and early twenties, but I wanted a job with a career path that didn't lead to fry cook. I decided there might be a decent future for me in a bank with a training program. I was both thrilled and nervous when I landed a job as secretary to a woman loan officer in the headquarters of a large bank. Having mainly worked in greasy spoons, I found the high rise building — all granite, chrome and elevators — pretty intimidating. A case of nerves probably caused me to start my period the night before my first day on the job. I put my hair in a conservative bun, put on a silk shirt and suit, and waddled my bloated little body off to work.

"By the morning coffee break, I had sweat rings under my armpits, my bun was straggling, and my tampon was flooding. I made my way to the enormous ladies room that had a long row of toilet stalls and a white tile floor. I replaced my tampon and flushed the toilet. Wouldn't you know it — I had chosen the one toilet that decided to malfunction that morning. I watched in horror as the bloody water rose higher and higher in the bowl. I had just made it to the sink when several women walked in the door, including my new boss. Their eyes all turned in unison to the rose-colored water now spilling onto the white tile. 'Somebody overflowed the toilet,' I blurted out. My boss told me to call the maintenance staff, as she watched 'somebody's' tampon float by."

*Tales of the Curse*

# The Morning After

"When my husband and I got married thirty-five years ago, we decided to splurge on a nice wedding and honeymoon rather than using our savings to buy a house right away. Like most brides back then, I wanted the whole episode to be a fairytale with me at the center. I planned everything from the fiber content of the wedding invitations to the recipe for the punch at the reception.

"My husband-to-be was in charge of the honeymoon because I was overwhelmed with life-or-death wedding decisions. So when my husband told me he planned a week in a bridal suite in Las Vegas, I was too swamped tying ribbons on groom's cakes and counting RSVP cards to interfere. He assured me all the details were covered. But what neither of us had the foresight to consider was coordinating the whole jamboree around my menstrual cycle. Fairytale princesses just don't have periods.

"The wedding day was hectic, but when we finally made it to our hotel with our luggage and nerves intact, we both lightened up. Our gaudy honeymoon suite was perfect. We felt like movie stars in our round velvet bed with a big crystal chandelier hanging from the mirrored ceiling. My husband had arranged for fresh roses and chilled champagne in the room, and our first night of marriage is a very romantic memory. But by morning, my honeymoon fantasy was brought to a screeching halt. We woke up to what looked like a scene from a slaughter house. We were both soaked with blood, and so were our pink satin sheets.

"We decided my husband would make a quick dash

for the shower, but then we realized that the big Jacuzzi we had filled with bubbles so happily the night before was the only fixture for bathing in the room. I stayed in bed continuing to drench the sheets while he stood waiting for the obscene tub to fill. He bathed, dressed, and went downstairs to search the casino for tampons. I knew right then that I had a great catch in this brave and loving man."

# Shopping Snafu

"In my twenties, my periods kept getting longer and longer and heavier and heavier. I was certain my life would eventually become an endless menstruation marathon. My poor husband was afraid I would become anemic. My doctor tried a few D and C treatments, but finally gave up. He advised me to hurry up and have my kids, then get a hysterectomy and be done with it.

"I followed his advice and had my two children, but I dragged my heels on the hysterectomy part. With two toddlers, the last thing I needed was to be recuperating from major surgery for six weeks. However, I got very motivated to have the operation after a mortifying shopping episode.

"It was a hot summer day, and I wore a light pair of shorts to the supermarket. With my little ones in tow, I was negotiating the aisles with my shopping cart, trying to distract the children from all the cleverly packaged junk food, when I realized that I had begun bleeding heavily. I abandoned my groceries in the middle of the store, dragged the confused kids to the car, and drove straight home to call my doctor and arrange for the surgery.

"During my recovery from the operation, I read an article in a women's magazine that was blasting doctors for doing way too many hysterectomies on women. But to me, saving a uterus after it has served its purpose is like saving eggshells or the empty seed packet after you plant the flower seeds. I say, good riddance to bad rubbish. I took my last box of tampons, tied tiny pink and blue ribbons around them, and celebrated my freedom by passing them out like cigars to all my girlfriends."

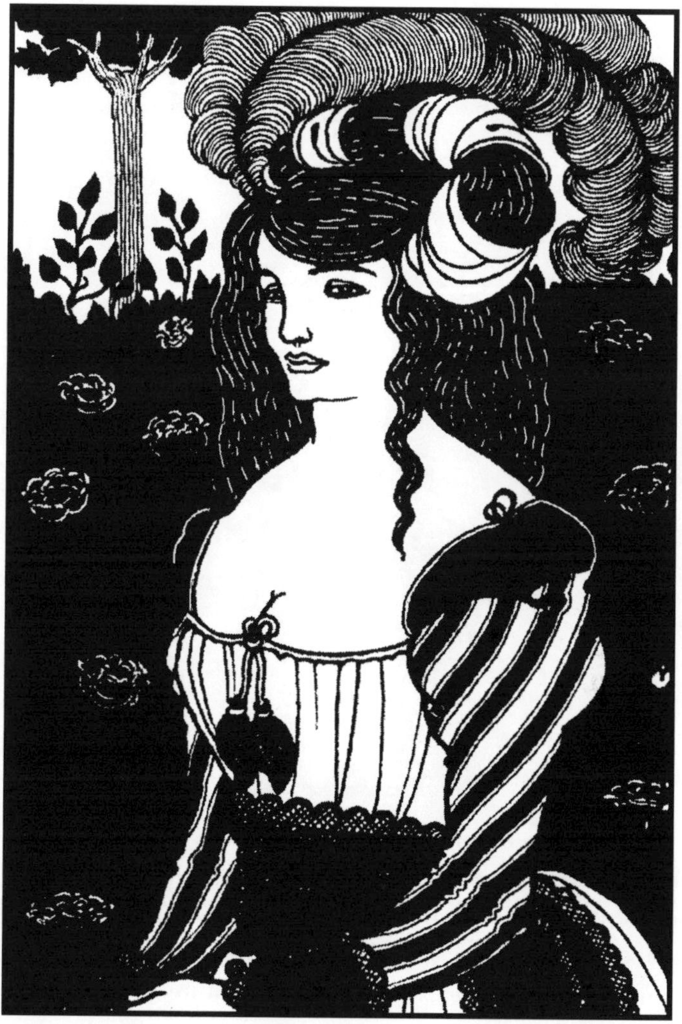

# Nowhere to Hide

Did you ever wonder what happens when a stripper has her period unexpectedly? This exotic dancer contributed her experience only after being assured that her story would be anonymous.

"One night before dancing, I was just walking around the crowded audience, chatting with people. I was wearing a white bra and thong and white heels. Suddenly I felt my period start with a gush.

"I sat down immediately on the closest chair, which I later discovered I was completely soaked. A sweet bartender came to my aid like an angel from heaven. I told him I needed a jacket, pronto. He went around to the tables looking for a man who would hand over his jacket, no questions asked. He returned quickly with a short red one which I rejected, and he continued his rescue mission. The next jacket he brought me was long enough to cover me adequately as I wriggled to the kitchen with my knees glued. Once in there, I dropped onto a vinyl-covered stool but could feel the seat immediately getting slippery. The kitchen workers were all Spanish-speaking guys, but they understood English well enough to get me some bar towels. I wasn't sure how to make it to the dressing room without making a huge mess and looking like a complete idiot, so I decided to wait until the flow lessened a bit.

"I sat in that state of living hell for an hour, which seemed like a year. Each time I stood up, it started all over again. My darling bartender canvassed the other dancers until he found a super tampon for me. By this time, the crew had cleared out of the kitchen. As soon as I heard the music signaling that another dancer was performing, I knew all eyes would be on her, and I took the opportunity to escape to the dressing room, using the towels to stem the tide. I can only imagine the cleanup job I left behind.

"All I know is that, from then on, I would just mention I was having my period, and I had all the time off I wanted. And there isn't anything I wouldn't do for that bartender who showed more kindness and was braver in a pinch than many a macho guy who comes to the strip club to escape into a fantasy world where a female dancer wouldn't dream of bleeding."

# Poppies in Bloom

"One of my favorite dresses from the sixties was a gorgeous summer evening gown just made for a party. Being a silk crepe, it draped perfectly against my body in graceful folds to the floor. It had huge red poppies on slender green stems scattered randomly across the chalk-white skirt, interspersed with the same blossom in white with just a fine black outline.

"I wore my gown to a close friend's evening wedding that had all the earmarks of becoming the event of the season. The impeccably groomed grounds of her parents' home were decorated with thousands of tiny lights, candles in tall hurricane lamps, and white roses everywhere.

"On a big stone terrace, rows and rows of director's chairs with white canvas seats were filled with guests in festive garb. The wedding march sounded, the bridal party entered, and under a glittering midsummer night sky, my friends were married in a lovely ceremony. Watching the newlyweds leave and head for the garden, my husband and I were among the last guests to leave the terrace.

"Some sixth sense made me look back at my vacated chair. To my horror, a huge red stain stared accusingly back at me from the pristine white canvas seat. I quickly grabbed several Kleenexes from my purse and spread them over the nasty spot.

"My heart sank at the thought that my dress would be ruined and I would have to 'back out' from the party. I grabbed the full skirt with both hands, rushed off to the powder room, and looked for the damage in the full-length mirror. Nothing! I saw no stain. However, a second, closer scrutiny revealed the addition of one more red poppy to the skirt. As though a careful hand had filled in the black outline, the once 'white' poppy was now as red as its neighbors. For once, the brutal red of a menstrual stain on a piece of white silk went unnoticed as I danced and swirled to the very end of the party."

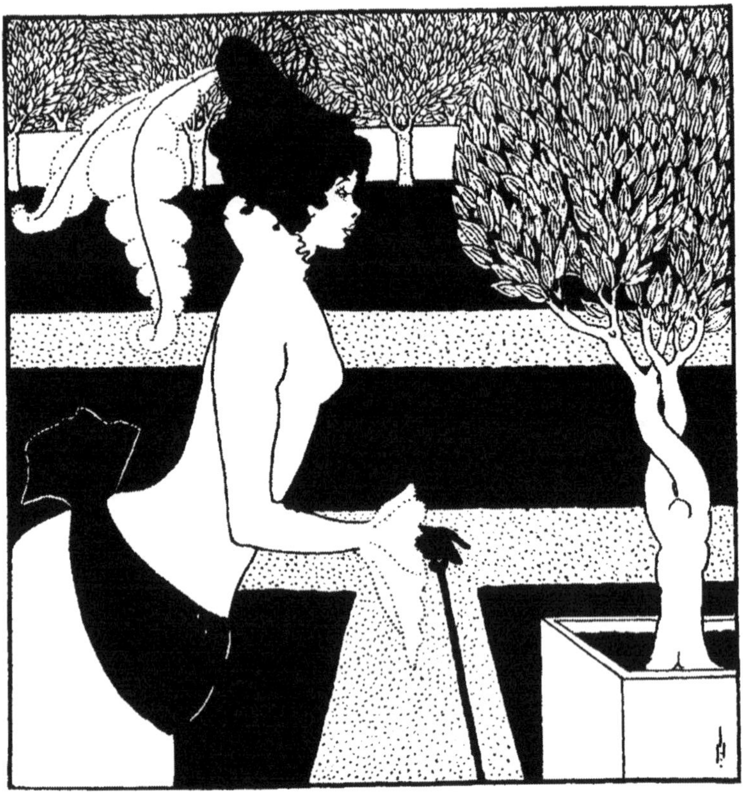

# Fly Your Flag

"On the day my friend Kathryn confided to me that she planned to end her fifteen-year marriage and I broke the news to her that I would soon be moving to Alaska, we decided such drastic life changes called for only one course of action — 'Let's go shopping!'

"We decided casual wear was a must for the long trip into Missoula, where a brand new mall was waiting for us. I threw on some jeans, a cotton blouse, and sandals, and Kathryn sported a pair of denim bib overalls with a bright blue T-shirt underneath. With her petite frame and childlike mannerisms, she looked more like a kid than the thirty-year-old woman she was. However, when you looked into her sapphire-blue eyes, you saw a deep intelligence, a sparkle of humor, and wisdom beyond her years — the ingredients of a truly beautiful woman.

"We grabbed our purses and headed out the door when Kathryn stopped dead in her tracks and said, 'Oh, nuts! I have to go grab a Kotex — just in case. I'll be right back.'

"She returned and jumped into the car, and we were on our way. Our drive to Missoula was a treat in itself. The majestic Rocky Mountains rose to touch the sky on either side of us as we drove along the Clark Fork River. We talked about our dreams as well as our fears. We marveled at the magic of friendship, the ups and downs of marriage, and the wonderment of motherhood. At times, we grew quiet, enchanted with the breathtaking scenery.

"Before we knew it, we had arrived — and we were shopping fools! We shopped and shopped, stopping only for a quick bite to keep our blood sugar up. Then back to the mall we went. We thoroughly ransacked a greeting card shop, giggling like schoolgirls at some of the risqué cards. We tried on shoes, hats, and scarves. The two of us kept at it until our feet were screaming and our pocketbooks were empty.

"Several times throughout the day we had noticed people looking at us oddly. We always laughed a lot when we were together, and this day was no exception. People just seemed to be laughing right along with us — or so we thought.

"Finally, we were totally spent. We'd had a perfect day. Just before leaving town, we decided to fill up the tank for the trip home. Kathryn pulled into a nearby gas station, hopped out, and began pumping gas. I noticed some teenage boys getting out of a truck behind her. They were pointing at her back and doing the 'red-faced giggle-and-snort.' When they had gone into the station, I quickly got out of the car to check out my friend's backside, just as she was replacing the gas nozzle — and there IT was. Sticking out of her back pocket, flapping as it had been throughout the entire day, waving like a flag in the breeze with every step she took, was her bright, white, 'just-in-case' Kotex — making its own statement to the world.

"We laughed until we cried and our bellies and faces ached. We went back over the day, remembering some of the odd looks we had received — and we started laughing all over again until we got home and were just too tired to laugh anymore. Twenty years later we still laugh until we cry every time we see each other and remember that special day."

# Finish Line

"I've often wondered if stress can bring on a period prematurely. When I was in high school, I was a 'miler' on the girls' track team. Just before a big track meet, I realized I was flowing and ran into the locker room. I had no pads or tampons, so I just folded layers of toilet paper and improvised. I felt pretty secure as I stretched and warmed up. And I wasn't even particularly worried when the starter's gun went off. But somewhere during the first lap, I realized my homemade pad was not very stable.

"By the time I reached the half-mile point, it had migrated from my crotch toward the back of my waistband. I was way too competitive to slow down and adjust it while I was racing. Besides, a runner sticking her hand in her britches would probably not go unnoticed by the spectators. I ignored my precarious condition and ran unprotected. Near the finish line, I accelerated past it and hightailed it to the locker room, never slowing or glancing around. When I finally returned to the field in my sweats, the coach announced my time: a new personal best."

# Trick or Treat

"Most of my memories about my periods are sad or painful, but there is one that stands alone. I went to a Halloween party in college dressed in a white majorette uniform. Sometime during the party, I realized I had begun to menstruate and had no supplies with me. As good fortune would have it, another woman came dressed in a gutsy costume. She wore a black sheath dress upon which she had vertically pasted row upon row of maxi-pads. When I asked her if I could borrow, or rather have one, she said, 'Nice try. Everyone has been coming up with that one.' When I finally convinced her I was seriously in need, she agreed to let me have one from under her arm area that didn't really show.

"When I told this story to a friend later, she laughed and told me a similar one. She had needed an emergency pad at a costume party once and, in a pinch, unraveled part of her husband's Egyptian mummy costume."

## Short Shorts

"It's strange how some of us run around like half-nude heathens today, and yet we still have Victorian attitudes about keeping our periods a secret. A few years ago, I was wearing a very short pair of fringed cutoffs, thinking I looked pretty hot. My boyfriend came over and tugged on a string that he thought was too long in the fringe. Unfortunately, it was the string to my tampon. We both nearly died.

"Either we must become more nonchalant about our bodies and their functions, or start dressing in bustles and floor length gowns to keep everything mysterious. It should be one way or the other."

# I Must Leave the Country Now

"My family lived about ninety miles from the ocean when I was in high school, and I begged my parents to let me go on a day trip to the beach with my friends. There was one special boy, Barry, who I knew would be going with the group. I thought he had been sending signals that conveyed his interest in me. He did special things like splashing water on me and pulling the back of my sweatshirt over my face. With overtures like that, it would be pretty hard not to notice that he liked me. The last car to take our group home was overcrowded. I volunteered to solve the problem by sitting on Barry's lap all the way back. When we arrived home and I got off his lap, we both noticed that I had started my period — on his jeans! I thought moving to Canada was not far enough away. Maybe Peru?"

# Naughty Bits

"One time I had a bloody nose at a cocktail party. Men and women alike rushed to my aid with all sorts of suggestions to make it stop. A friend put a cold cloth on the back of my neck and made me tilt my head back. People checked with me all evening long to see how I was doing. It was a communal event. But, at another party, I started my monthly flow and leaked through my silk jumpsuit. From the reaction of both men and women, you would have thought I had just peed on the carpet. Why was that so different from the nosebleed that got me nothing but sympathy? It was probably about the same amount of blood. I guess it's because menstrual blood is from 'the private place,' the one that is not supposed to be spoken of except by doctors or pornographers. Oh, the dark, dark secrets of the female mystique!"

# Pinch Hitting

Women report using a wide variety of substitutes when they don't have any tampons or pads on hand. Here are a few I have heard of:

- toilet paper
- paper towels
- cotton balls
- Kleenex
- socks
- neckties
- handkerchiefs
- sponges
- rags
- table napkins
- dishtowels
- diapers

Conversely, the old-style Kotex has been found being put to creative use as a:

- splint for cropped Doberman pinscher's ears
- glass cleaner
- sweatband for a construction worker's forehead
- way to stop the dripping sound of a leaky faucet
- Barbie doll mattress

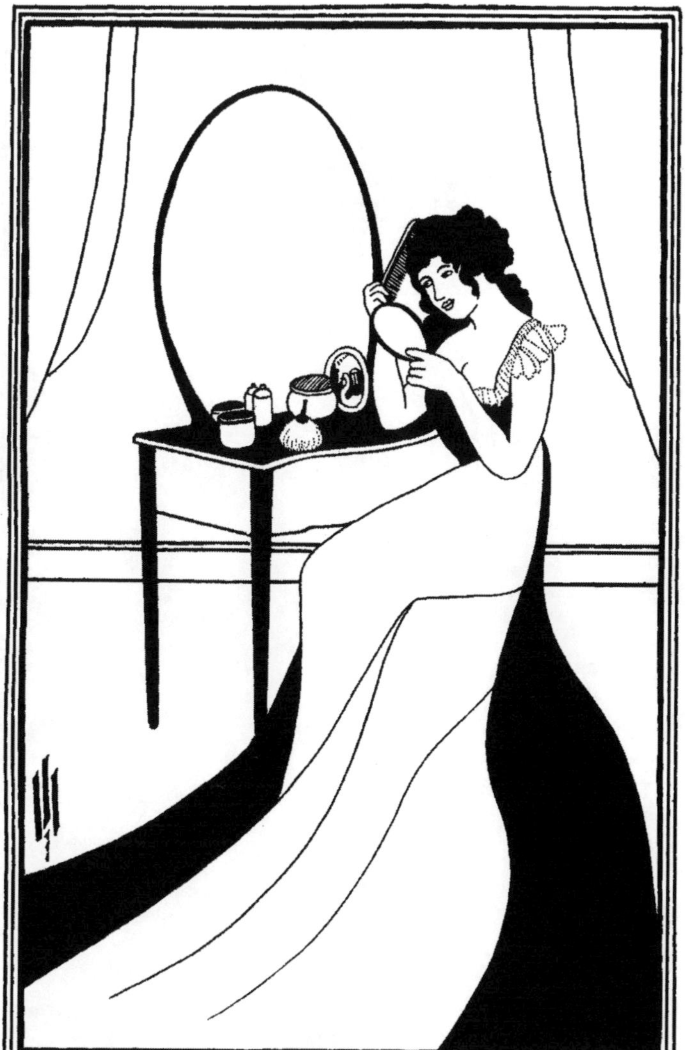

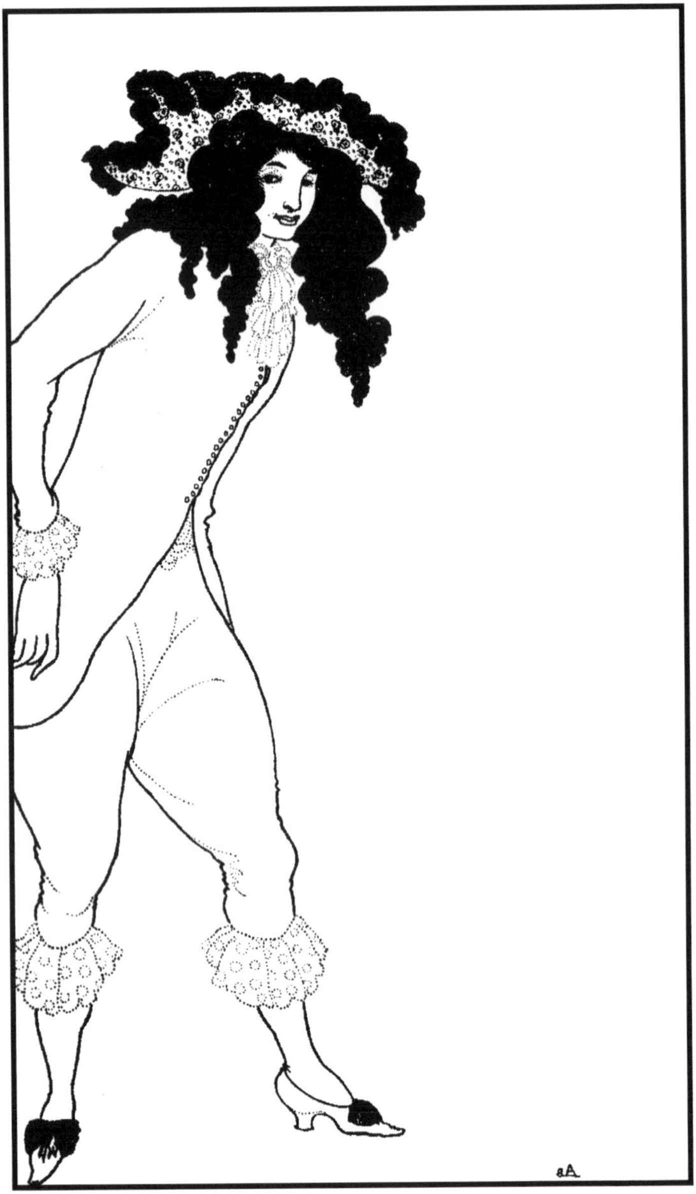

# Part Two
# The Men in Menstruation

For many women, the actions and attitudes of the males in their lives substantially influence whether their menstrual experiences are a pain or a privilege; whether they become a pariah or a princess. In this part, we hear women tell of their heroes and demons, and we also hear stories from a few men who were brave enough to share their own foibles.

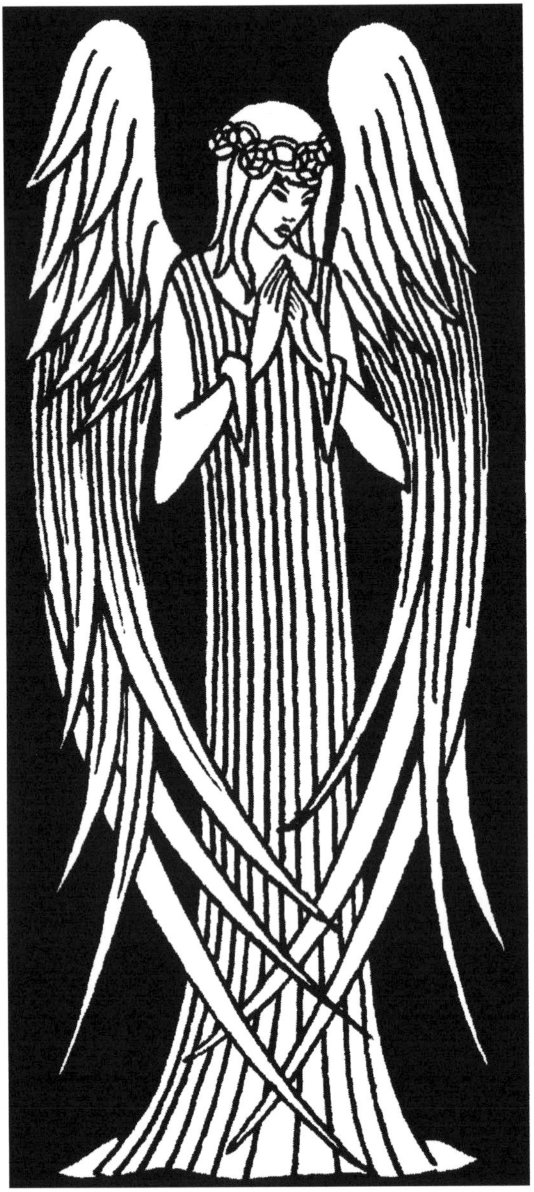

# God Must Be a Guy

"It doesn't seem fair that one woman ate one little apple in the Garden of Eden, and the rest of us women were doomed to suffer the Curse of Eve forever. As a little girl in Bible school reading Leviticus 15, in which Moses passes along the rules from God, I wondered what horrible deed 'menstruate' might be:

*When a woman menstruates, she shall be in a state of ceremonial defilement for seven days afterwards, and during that time anyone touching her shall be defiled until evening. Anything she lies on or sits on during that time shall be defiled. Anyone touching her bed or anything she sits upon shall wash his clothes and bathe himself and be ceremonially defiled until evening. A man having sexual intercourse with her during this time is ceremonially defiled for seven days, and every bed he lies upon shall be defiled...*

*On the eighth day, she shall take two turtledoves or two young pigeons and bring them to the priest at the entrance of the Tabernacle, and the priests shall offer one for a sin offering and the other for a burnt offering, and make atonement for her before the Lord, for her menstrual defilement.*

"When I found out what the word 'menstruates' meant, I started to get an inkling that God must not be a woman. And when I started my periods at thirteen, I was convinced God is a man, because a woman would never do that to her own kind."

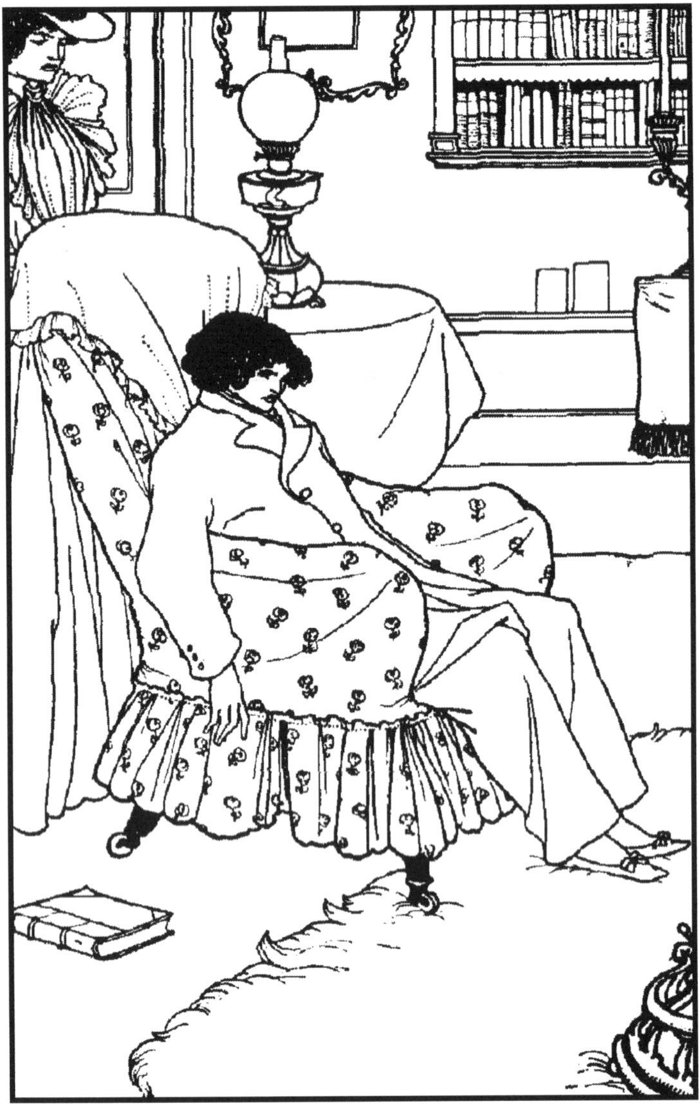

# House of Estrogen

"Having a mother and three older sisters in the household probably accounts partially for my kid brother's warped personality. With four females having their periods every month, he learned at a young age about the big plastic bag, nicknamed the 'Kotex Bag,' that served as the receptacle for our used sanitary supplies in our only family bathroom. One day the squirrelly kid used it as an instrument of vengeance against me after I had committed the unpardonable sin of tattling to Mom that he had stashed a whole bag of chocolate chips in his underwear drawer. I would never have discovered his loot had I not been searching for a pair of his gym socks to fill out my new Circlette brassiere. Using my own lummox-size socks would have boosted me to a double D-cup, and of course I didn't want to look cheap. The chocolate theft landed my brother the supreme penalty of doing dishes single-handedly for a whole week. I felt a trace of compunction about ratting him out, but it was just so satisfying at the time. Needless to say, the sibling rivalry code mandated that he, in turn, be allowed a free 'I'll get you for that.' But I'm stunned to this day by how he got even.

"I had just entered the wonderful world of dating in high school, and through an elaborate set of cafeteria-line negotiations, I landed an invitation to a movie with someone who qualified in my book as a neat guy. (Translation: someone my friends wanted.) He was the class treasurer, a fact I played up to the hilt in pleading with my parents to let me go out with him. But the real attraction was that he had a driver's license and his own car, which was mostly one color and whose dents barely showed. My parents finally relented, if only to stop my whining from drowning out the television. But they insisted on meeting him and imposing a humiliating curfew. Despite the hurdles, I was ready and waiting in my single-sock facsimile of a C-cup when my date arrived at the door. After the stiff introductions and mandatory warnings, we stepped out the front door to make our escape and heard the voice of my brother taunting, 'Yoo-hoo, yoo-hoo.' He was hanging out the window over the front door, swinging the Kotex Bag, trying to look menacing. I honestly don't think he meant to swing it quite so hard, but he lost his hold on the bag. The dreaded contents spilled out and showered down upon me and my date. My brother vanished instantly and I, in shock, simply refused to acknowledge what had happened.

"I immediately asked my date what movie we were going to see, and he gladly went along and ignored the reality of our situation, escorting me politely down the littered sidewalk. Apparently he had his heart set on having a proper date as much as I did. By the time he brought me home, there was no sign of the bag or its loathsome contents. I guess my brother sneaked outside before my parents saw the mess and picked everything up. That in itself had to be ample punishment for any boy, so I never retaliated. Knowing that he had crossed an unacceptable line with me, from then on my brother redirected his harassment to my sisters. But the cosmic law of atonement cannot be escaped, and today my brother is a grown man with a little boy just like him."

# From the Mouths of Babes

"My son Rick was almost six years old and his sister Molly age three, when the golden opportunity for teaching sex education presented itself. Rick asked, 'Mom, Mrs. Brooks said that when we die we go to Heaven. Did I come from Heaven?'

"Brown eyes looked trustingly up at me — ME, the source of wisdom, clean clothes, and cookies. Without a moment's hesitation I headed for my stash of Golden Books and other sex education materials that I had hoarded for just this moment. I called Molly away from her coloring project to join her brother, and we settled down on the living room floor.

"'It's story time,' I announced cheerfully, and I had their attention immediately. Since I taught them everything from brushing their teeth to table manners, I wanted them to hear the magical story of LIFE in my words — my way.

"The afternoon just flew by. We covered the topics of boys' penises, girls' vaginas, having babies, and menstruation. We talked about responsibility, what it took to be a parent, and how important it was to honor ourselves, as well as life and its generous gifts. I discovered how easy it was to talk to my young children about a taboo subject because to them it was just another wonderful story — devoid of smut, innuendo and nasty secrets. My husband and I didn't believe in secrets, especially when it concerned the human body and its functions.

"Several months passed, and every once in a while instead of reading a story at bedtime, Molly and Rick wanted

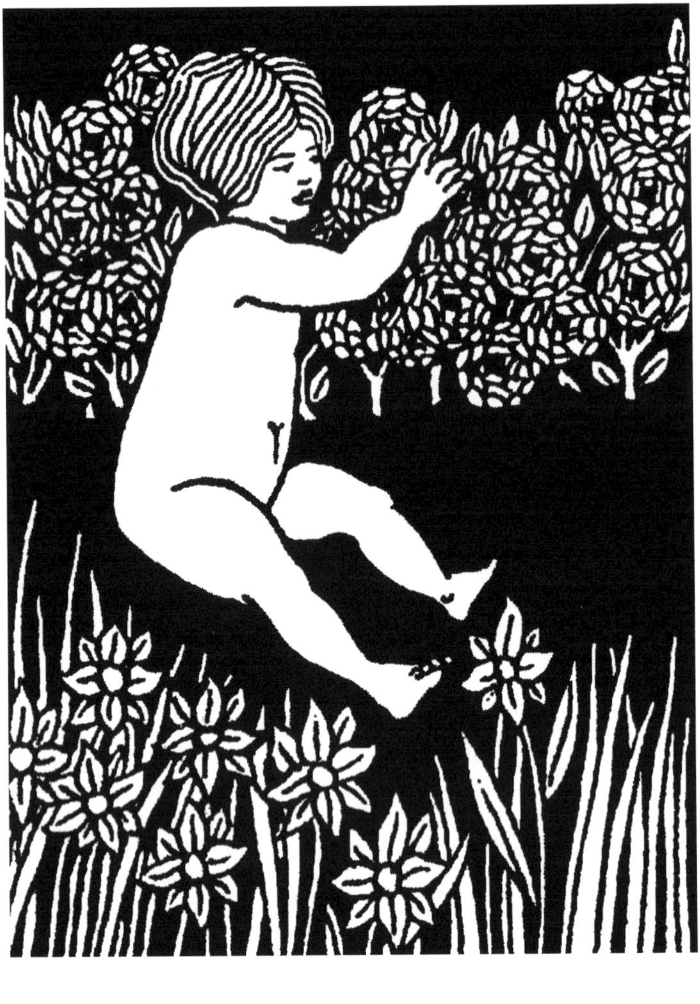

to hear again about the wonderful time when they lived inside me. The magic and awe of creation remained a source of joy. There were no moments of embarrassment.

"One day, the mailman rang the doorbell and I asked Molly, now four years old, to get the door as I disappeared into the bathroom with my newly purchased super-economy-size box of Kotex. I told her I would be right there.

"When I appeared at the open front door, there stood the mailman rooted to the porch, staring at Molly. With Mom on hand, she returned to playing with a friend in her room, unaware of the mailman's expression of consternation.

"When I asked him what was wrong he whispered, 'Well, I, I think you need to know what your daughter just said to me when I said I needed to see you about some postage due.'

"He was uncomfortable and hesitant as he went on, 'Well, um, she told me that you couldn't come to the door because you were changing a K-k-ko-t-tex.' He finally got the shameful word out of his mouth.

"Relieved that there was no real problem, I laughed and said, 'If you don't know all about menstruation at your age you'd better come in, and I'll give you a quick run-through on the subject.'

"'Oh, no!' he managed to squeak, shaking his head, blushing vividly and beating a quick retreat down the steps. That was the last I saw of him. From then on, he avoided all contact with me, even if it meant paying my postage-due out of his own pocket!"

# Interiors by Junior

"My kid is going to grow up to be an interior decorator, or maybe a set designer. But in the meantime, I may have trouble maintaining my sanity. Ever since he was old enough to walk, he has 'decorated' our house in themes. One fall he brought in leaves from the yard and arranged them all over the dining room. One day, he pulled up my pansies by the roots and put them all around the Jacuzzi in little Dixie cups plastered with unused postage stamps. Another time, he found spools of my gift wrapping ribbon and decorated Daddy's garage. He also thought my fancy underwear was ornamental enough to adorn the Christmas tree one year. But he really went over the top when he was six years old and I was having a Junior League committee meeting at my home.

"I had fussed and fumed over each little detail in the house, fluffing every last sofa pillow until I captured that casually elegant effect. I put on a little silk dress, brewed Starbucks coffee, and set the stage to look like *Better Homes and Gardens*. The ladies arrived, and the meeting went along just fine until one of the women excused herself to visit 'the little girls' room.'

"She opened the door to the powder room, gave out an unladylike yelp, and slammed the door shut. I didn't have the courage to ask her what was wrong, but I knew I had to open that door and face whatever was the problem. If that kid had used the toilet and not flushed again, after all my nagging, I would just have to strangle him. I was almost relieved when I opened the door and saw his latest bizarre creation. Junior had found a case, not just a box mind you, of my maxi-pads. He had taken every last pad, peeled off the protective paper strips, and proceeded to plaster every available surface in the room with maxi-pads. He hadn't just stuck them around randomly. He made flower designs on the cabinets and walls and mirror. He tucked the adhesive strips under the toilet seat to make a kind of fringe.

"What if he ends up being a world famous artist and I'm asked for samples of his early works for posterity? I should have taken pictures of his powder room art. But, in typical parental fashion, I failed to appreciate the great art for what it was. At the time, I just thought I was the mother of a demon seed who was out to get me."

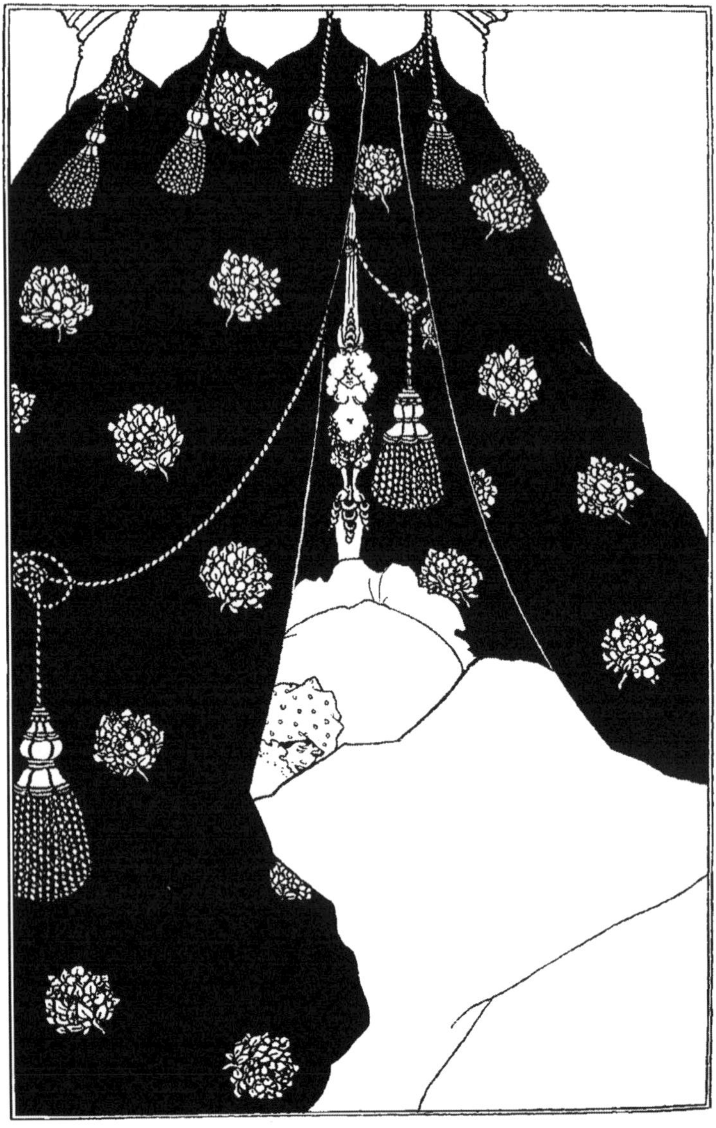

# It's a Bird, It's a Plane, It's Midol Man

A publisher fondly remembers the strange way he became a hero to his ten-year-old buddies.

"One day, a girl in my fifth-grade class gave me a rare piece of contraband — a Midol — which I immediately showed off to my friends. That night, all the boys came over to my house with their sleeping bags. We stared at that Midol for hours, daring each other to take it. Finally, I agreed to be the guinea pig. Witnessed by my wide-eyed audience, I swallowed the pill, not wanting to be labeled a chicken. I knew this act of bravery would put me in a league of my own on the playground.

"When I had no immediate reaction to the Midol, the guys kept vigil with me all night long, waiting for some mysterious process to start. Not one eye closed, for fear of missing the change I would undergo. When morning finally came, we rolled up our sleeping bags in a sleep-deprived stupor, disappointed and yet somewhat relieved that I was the same old me. Who knows what could have happened? I could have been the first boy in history to have a period. I could have grown breasts. Or worse yet, I could have started throwing the ball like a girl!"

# Sweet Bird of Youth

"Perhaps the biggest upset of my children's life was the day they found an injured robin. When they ran into the house to break the news of their discovery to my wife and me, I didn't want to tell them that the culprit was probably their beloved cat, Lucky, who would pounce on anything that moved. While my daughter Jessica kneeled beside the bird, hands over her heart, imploring the Heavens to intercede on behalf of God's wounded little creature, my son Justin tried to force-feed water into its beak with an eyedropper.

"When his poking and prodding no longer yielded any response from the bird, my son officially pronounced him 'past-a-way' and notified us that he and Jessica would prepare a funeral service in the backyard. When Jessica came to escort us outside for the proceedings, she gathered us in front of the altar, which had heretofore been their swing set. As Jessica solemnly sang 'This Little Light of Mine,' Justin gravely brought forth the little bird corpse, festooned with dandelions, and lying in state upon a Super Kotex Maxi-Pad.

"My wife and I squeezed each other's hand and summoned every ounce of self-control. The tears we shed were from stifled laughter, not grief, as Justin assured God that this had been 'a very good bird who you would want to have in Heaven.' Justin looked at us and said, 'You may place the "diseased" in the grave now,' pointing to the little hole he had dug under the slide. My wife, failing to see the similarity between this and throwing a few chicken parts on the barbecue, gave me a look as if to say 'I'm not touching that thing.' But I must admit, for some reason the thought of picking up that Kotex sent a shudder through my own spine. So in the end, I picked up the bird by a wing and motioned to my wife, who then put the Kotex in the hole, whereupon I gingerly placed the ill-fated robin onto his final, sanitary and super-absorbent, resting place."

# Beloved Wimp

"It's great to be able to talk about this, even if it is anonymously, because I've never been able to tell anyone without humiliating my dear husband. He's one great guy, but he has a squeamish side. Like when he came to see me in the hospital after I had just delivered our daughter (no way he could be in the delivery room) the nurse came into the room to give me a measles shot. The hypodermic needle got within a foot of my arm and my husband started to swoon. He barely staggered out of the room, and the nurse had to go tend to him before she could give me the shot. So needless to say, I always try to conceal everything about my monthly periods from Mr. Hit-the-Deck. I just mention that I'm 'out of commission,' and he keeps his distance until I give him the all clear signal.

"But one month, I was feeling frisky and didn't realize the date was dangerously close to when my period would be due. Something about the hormones must have really put me in a sexy mood. Hubby was delighted, and neither of us noticed anything unusual. But afterward, he walked from the dark bedroom into the bathroom and turned on the light.

"All I heard was the thud. I kept calling, 'Honey, Honey,' but didn't hear anything. So I climbed out of bed and went into the bathroom. Apparently, I had started my period, and when he turned on the bathroom light and looked down to see the blood on himself, my husband passed out cold on the tile floor. I cleaned him up before shaking him awake. He got up and said, 'Must have slipped.' He had some pretty good bruises the next day, but we never spoke of it again."

# A Gallant Geek

"It's hard to understand what made us think certain fads were cool in junior high school, but during my eighth-grade year in the late fifties, I was the very proud owner of a purse that looked like a decorative box. The top of the purse was actually a lid with a hinged wooden handle, and it was adorned with pieces of genuine mother-of-pearl. In it I neatly stored all of my necessary equipment for a day at junior high: lunch money, a rabbit's-foot key chain with several unidentified keys, a number-two Dixon pencil, a Pink Pearl eraser, a piece of binder paper upon which I had documented the *Hit Parade* songs for the week, a Cutex lipstick in my signature shade of Champagne Pink, a rattail comb for my bubble-cut hairdo, and sitting on top where it would be handy, a nice clean change of Kotex.

"Still being the class tomboy, when it was recess time I was the first one out of the classroom. I had a standing game of dodge ball and didn't want to be late when teams were chosen. So, I tore out of the room as soon as the bell rang, leaving my precious purse safely sitting on top of my desk with its lid securely latched. But when I came back into the room after recess, I was horrified to see that the lid of my purse was ajar. In fact, it looked as though the hinges were sprung. Now, a woman guards her purse as ferociously as the alpha lion guards his territory, and woe be unto the person who violates it. I was both angry over the obvious travesty and somehow guilty about the contents.

"Behind my desk sat a runt of a boy, who didn't run with the pack because his voice hadn't changed, his upper lip was still hairless, and his hormones weren't compelling him yet to be sufficiently obnoxious to be noticed by the girls. In other words, we classified him as a geek, dork, dink, nerd, or any of the other words we used for people who were kind. When he saw the look on my face, he explained that, as everyone was rushing out of the room, my desk had been bumped, knocking my purse on the floor and sending its contents flying. He said he had picked up the purse and put my 'stuff' back into it as discreetly as possible. I scanned his face for any trace of a mocking smile, but all I saw was sincere concern.

"There never was a peep from any other classmate about the incident, and I know they would have had a field day had he ever mentioned it to any of them. And these many years later, that simple act of kindness stands alone in all my memories of junior high school, where humiliation of our peers was perfected to an art form. I hope today that guy has a loving wife who appreciates his tact and sensitivity. If he does, I'll bet he even goes to the store and buys tampons for her, because that guy was one in a million."

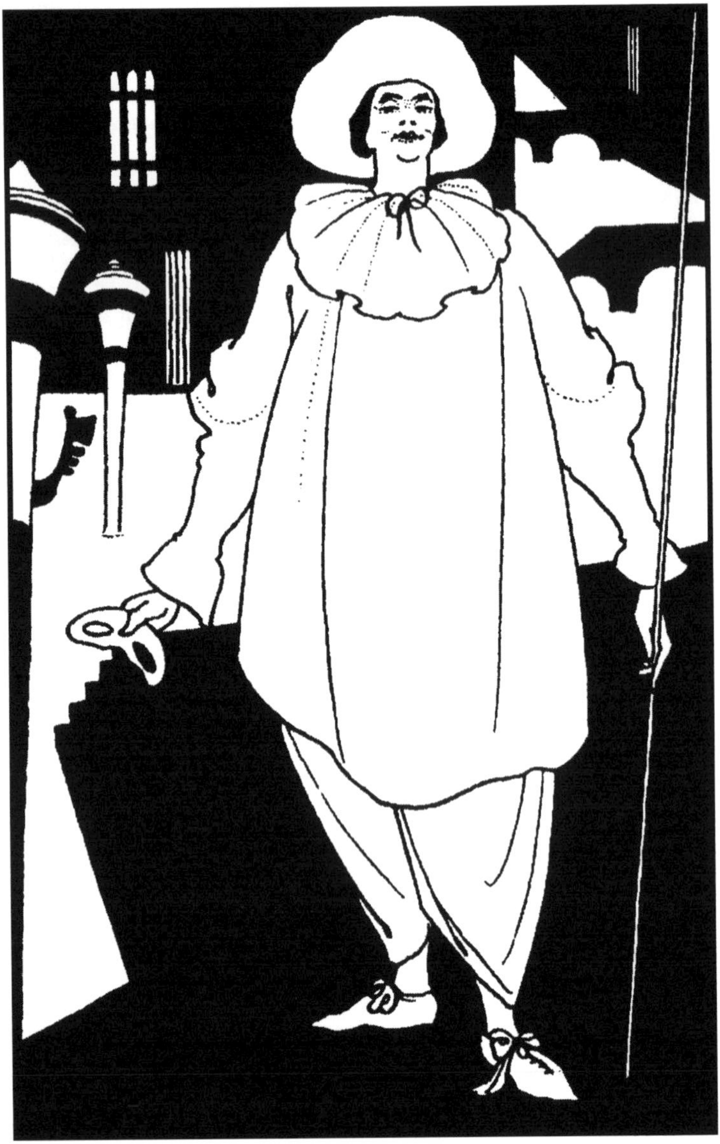

# Poker Faces

"I started my period at age ten while I was horseback riding. When I came into the house to use the bathroom and discovered blood, I ran to tell Mother, thinking I had jarred something loose by riding too hard. She explained what was happening to me so matter-of-factly that I just didn't think it was any big deal. She gave me a sanitary belt and some Kotex and sent me back out riding. Her manner did not convey to me the notion that periods or Kotex would be a taboo subject, but I found out the contrary that night.

"I was in the basement playing, and I gouged my arm on an exposed nail. The cut wasn't deep, but it was several inches long and bleeding a little. I ran upstairs and grabbed a Kotex, thinking it would make a perfect bandage if I tied the tails around my arm. But I couldn't manage to tie it with one hand, so I ran into the kitchen where Daddy was having his weekly poker game with his buddies. I asked him if he could tie the Kotex for me. For such supposedly good poker players, the guys sure didn't do a good job of keeping straight faces. I learned from their varying degrees of embarrassment and horror that I was now in an arena that men didn't particularly care to know about."

AB.

# Having a Blast

A dentist and oral surgeon stretched the Hippocratic oath a bit when he first began practicing:

"I enlisted for a two-year stint in the Army right out of dental school, so my patients were primarily nineteen-year-old recruits who usually didn't have a great deal of worldly experience. One rookie came to my office with his freshly shaven head and his government-issue fatigues and sat in my chair for what may have been his first dental visit ever. It was clear that he and his toothbrush were not on intimate terms. He needed a wake-up call to get him to start taking care of his sadly neglected teeth. I took the Army nurse who was assisting me into another room and asked her if by any chance she had a tampon handy. She did, and I brought her in as an accomplice to my scheme.

"Back in the procedure room, I gravely explained to the patient that his long-term neglect of his teeth had left me with only one option. 'We're going to have to blast,' I said with a deadpan face. I put the tampon between his teeth, told him to bite down, and then lit the string hanging out of his mouth with a lighter. His eyes popped open in terror as the nurse and I ran for cover. Our giggling in the hallway gave us away, and the recruit spit out the tampon, unable to cuss me out properly because I was a superior officer. (Profanity must follow the one-way chain of command.) I told him if he didn't start taking care of his teeth every day, I would have to pull out every tooth in his head. He got the message."

# A Cop Stopper

"One awesome summer morning, I put the top down on my convertible, turned on the oldies-but-goodies radio station, and headed my car in the direction of the beach. I was blithely bouncing along to the tune of 'Born to Be Wild' when a flashing light in my rear view mirror made my foot spontaneously hit the brake pedal. Too late I realized my speedometer needle was on the wrong side of eighty miles an hour. Sweat broke out all over me as I pulled dutifully over to the curb, wondering if my tank top and little shorts would be warm enough when the officer hauled me off to a cold jail cell.

"I peeled myself off the leather seat and got out of the car to get my driver's license from my bag in the trunk. As the hulking patrolman lumbered toward me, dripping with hardware, he looked like Mr. Universe dressed for a S.W.A.T. maneuver. He was equipped to take down a pack of Hell's Angels or an international drug cartel as he asked for my driver's license and vehicle registration. His shadow fell over me as I nervously fumbled through my bag searching for my license.

"Apparently, the stress of the situation caused my period to start at that most inopportune moment. When I felt the blood trickling down my leg, I automatically spread my knees a little and looked down. The officer, being keenly alert to body language, followed my gaze. His face went red as Mr. Macho suddenly became a puddle of warm Jello. He recovered enough to tell me to slow down and always use my safety belt before he fled to the sanctuary of his patrol car. He burned rubber as he peeled away from the curb, lights flashing and siren wailing, off to some presumed emergency.

"I couldn't help but chuckle at this brave policeman who daily faced bullets and knives, killers and crooks, but lost it at the sight of a little blood — menstrual blood that is."

# Excuse Me!

"I'm a fourth grade teacher, and some of my students know the facts of life and some do not. Most of the kids get the scoop on the playground, straightened out later by the puberty film they eventually see in school. But I try to be careful about the terms I use so I don't get sniggering chaos in the classroom. My school has a rule that the teacher can never leave the classroom unattended, which can be a major annoyance when your period hits you by surprise. The only way of communicating with the office is through the public address system, so the female faculty and the school secretary have a code system to let her know when we need someone to cover our classroom while we hightail it to the tampon machine in the ladies room.

"One day, while I was barely maintaining control over the inevitable pandemonium as my little darlings made Zuni masks out of papier-mâché, I realized I needed to leave the classroom. Unfortunately, when I called in on the PA system, I got the ear of our somewhat obtuse male principal who was apparently not privy to the code. I told him I needed relief, but he didn't know what I was talking about. I gave it another stab and said I needed someone to cover the classroom for a few minutes. He said he could come in twenty minutes. I told him I needed someone right away. He wanted to know why. A pint-sized voice piped up from the class, ''Cuz she started her period.'

"The only face redder than mine was the principal's when he broke a land speed record to come and relieve me."

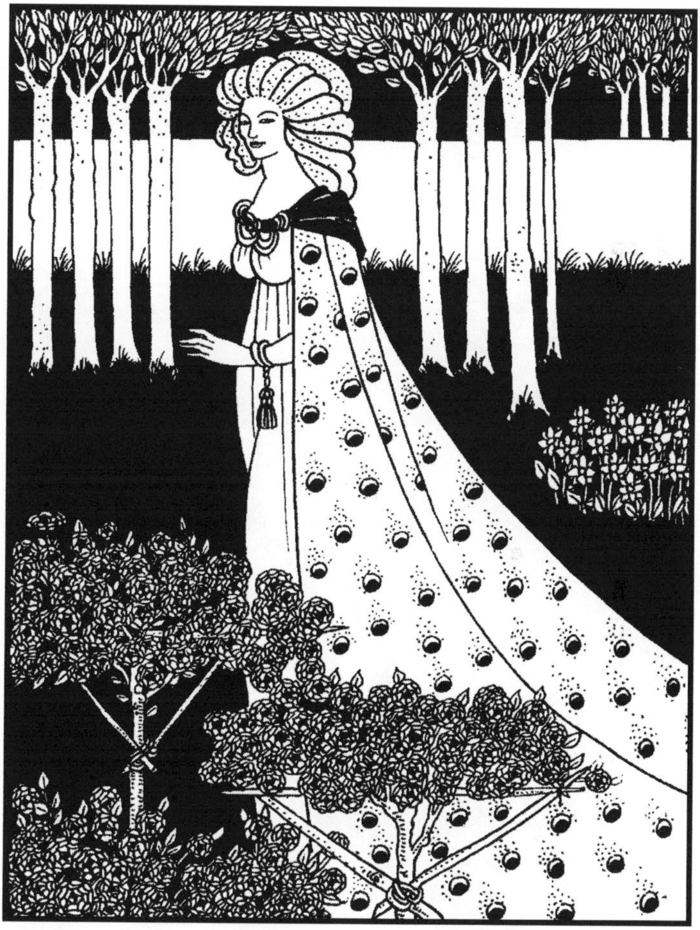

# For the Man Who Has Everything

"My husband and I were invited to the sixtieth birthday party of one of my father's close business associates. Spoiled, wealthy, and elegant beyond words, Eric resided in a treasure-filled mini-mansion. His little palace had been featured in all the prestigious architectural magazines and had won high praise for its magnificent decor and furnishings. Feature writers fawned over his unerring good taste, his extensive library of first editions, and his priceless collection of French Impressionist art.

"In spite of all his wealth and his place in *haute monde*, the man was lonely and there was nothing he loved better than attention, a party, and gifts. Browsing at one of my favorite antique stores, I came across a beautiful ivory box — slightly larger than a brick, with an exquisitely carved lid and a price tag I could afford. It was a beautiful piece — the kind that makes a rich man feel richer.

"At home, my daughter and I cleared the kitchen table to wrap the ivory box, along with several other presents for the upcoming birthdays of some uncles and cousins. To honor the lovely gift, we chose a silky paper with an Oriental design and a gorgeous, wide satin ribbon for the utmost touch of luxury.

"Carried away with wrapping fever, my daughter jokingly wrapped a newly purchased box of Tampax with some of the leftover paper and finished her handiwork with the satin ribbon.

"Her eyes sparkling with mischief, she said, 'Here, a gift for the woman who has everything.' Her voice gave way to giggles, which quickly turned into infectious laughter, as she handed me the well-dressed box of sanitary supplies.

"I joined in the merrymaking and handed the glamorous-looking gift back to Missy, instructing her to take it to my bathroom. I told her to put the birthday packages in the big 'outgoing' basket in the hall, and I left the kitchen. We always checked the contents of the hall basket before leaving the house. It held everything that one of us might have to take along — from umbrellas to gifts, mail, library books or an express package.

"Before leaving the house to attend Eric's birthday party, I dipped down into the basket on the floor, retrieved the beautifully wrapped box with the satin ribbon, and we were on our way to the festivities.

"After a lavish dinner, a round of rousing toasts, and tons of good wishes, we retired to the spacious living room where our beaming host tore into his packages with child-like glee. Friends had outdone themselves to find something unique for the man who already had everything. When Eric reached for our present from the table next to him, I couldn't take my eyes off him. I just knew he would love it. He stripped off the ribbon, tore at the restraining wrapping paper and revealed, to my great horror, the box of Tampax.

"Eric looked bewildered. His head whipped back as though he'd been slapped in the face, and he dropped the offensive box to the floor like a hot piece of coal. The room grew silent as a tomb, except for one nervous titter. I gasped for air like a fish out of water, mentally throttling my darling daughter. In a flash, I rushed to his side, grabbed the box and the wrappings with one hand, reached for another gift from the table, and handed it to my host. I mumbled something unintelligible under my breath and made a mad dash for the powder room, where I deposited the misdirected gift in the cupboard under the sink.

"Later in the evening, when the mood was festive once again, I approached Eric and told him my story. He had sufficiently recovered and graciously insisted on forgetting the matter. However, would I bring by the right present the next day? Please?"

# The Unflappable Gourmet

"My husband and I were invited to dinner at the home of close friends. Our hostess was a fabulous cook who liked to have her guests sit and visit with her while she cooked her gourmet dinners. Whether it was the heat of the kitchen or too many cocktails, I don't know, but my husband developed a nosebleed before dinner. He just couldn't get it to stop. Dinner was ready, and he couldn't eat and hold a tissue to his nose at the same time. So our hostess went to her bathroom, brought back a tampon, and stuck it up my husband's nostril. It worked like a charm to stop the bleeding. He just had to be careful not to bite the string when he ate. The dinner was delicious, but I developed a bad case of indigestion from laughing and chewing at the same time when I saw him trying to seriously discuss politics with that thing up his nose."

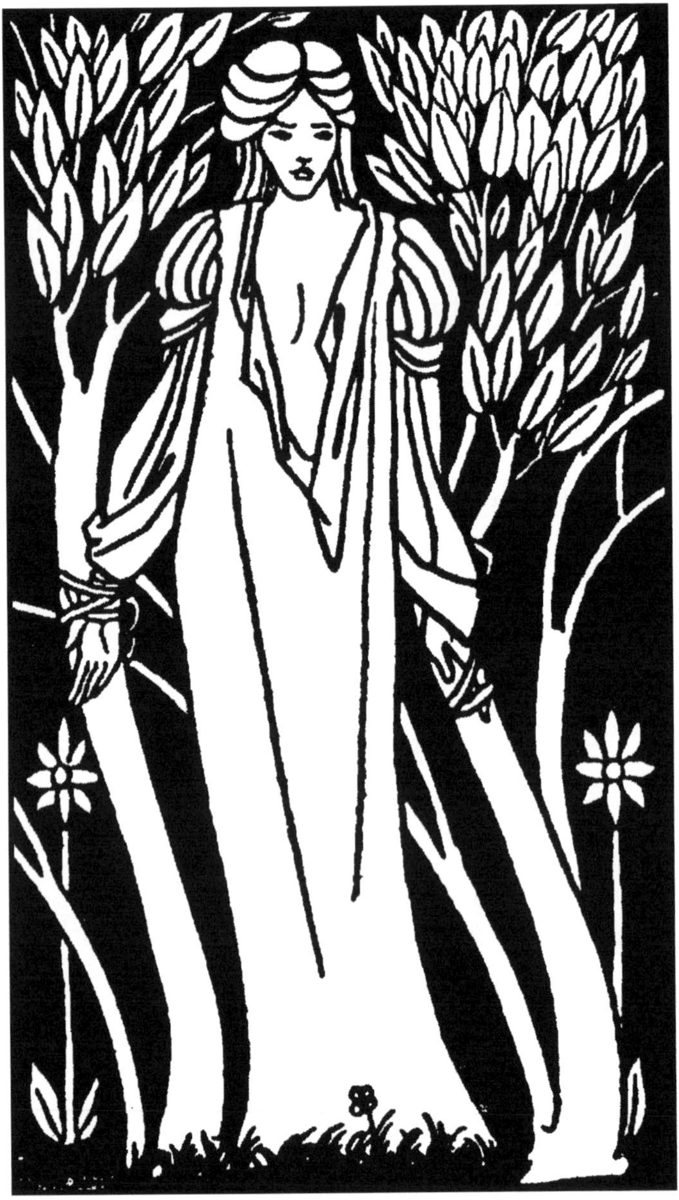

# The Punching Bag

"This may be just a coincidence, but I used to have terrible monthly cramps the whole time I was married. Sometimes, I thought maybe I was trying to get even with my husband because he used to rough me up whenever he drank too much, which was anytime he drank at all. My friends told me over and over that I was such a saint. For years we went on this way, with me scoring points with friends and family for being the poor victim, and him feeling guilty and getting mad because I let him do it to me.

"Eventually, I ended up in the hospital one night, leaving my husband, the drunk, to take care of the kids, who were scared to death. I'll never forget one nurse in the emergency room. One look at my injuries and she knew exactly what had happened. I thought for sure she would comfort me, because I was pretty shaken up. But instead she said, 'When are you going to stand up and be a woman and show your kids the right way to live?'

"That was just what I needed to hear. It was the beginning of my independence. My husband wouldn't go to counseling, and he sure as hell wouldn't stop drinking. So the next time he laid a hand on me, I called the cops. They let him cool down overnight in jail and put me in touch with a crisis center. The kids and I are on public assistance for a little while, just until I finish my vocational training.

"For whatever reason, I don't have monthly cramps anymore. I'm not saying my husband caused them. But once I broke free of my hurtful husband, the other pain went away too."

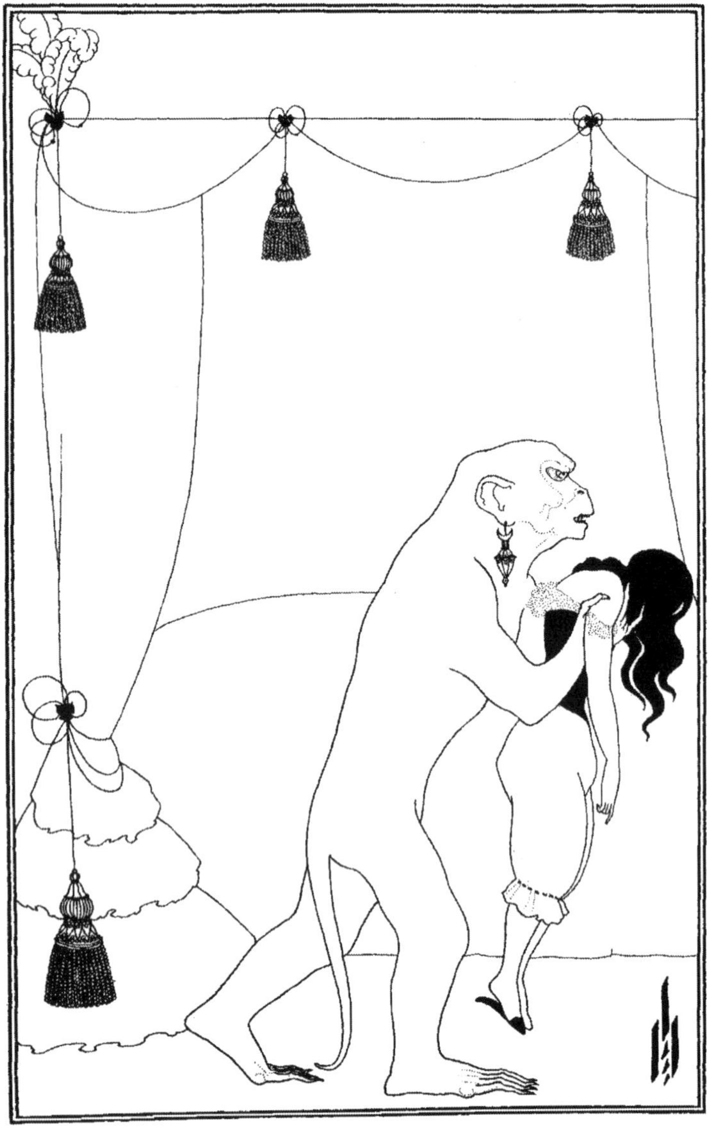

# My Monthly Monster Man

This story is submitted by a French Canadian who adds, "Laugh therapy, or *rigolotherapie* as we say in French, is an excellent way to prevent illness or to make pain more bearable." She also uses another technique:

"For years I couldn't figure out why my husband turned into a monster every month. As a young bride of twenty, I would get into fights with my monster husband that would reverberate throughout the entire apartment complex. They are still talked about today. I would throw his things into a big garbage bag and then throw the bag over the balcony. I would send him back to his mother's house, screaming that I wanted a divorce. Soon, he wouldn't seem like such a monster, and I would let him move back to the apartment. When articles began to appear in newspapers and magazines about PMS, it slowly began to dawn on me that my husband's monstrous periods coincided with my monthly cycle. Could it be possible that I was the one causing the chaos? Could this mysterious PMS be the culprit?

"Now that I am older, and maybe a little wiser, I am still not immune to PMS. I still get whopper cases. But nowadays, I drain off the hormone excess on a punching bag. No, not my husband: I use a real punching bag at the gym."

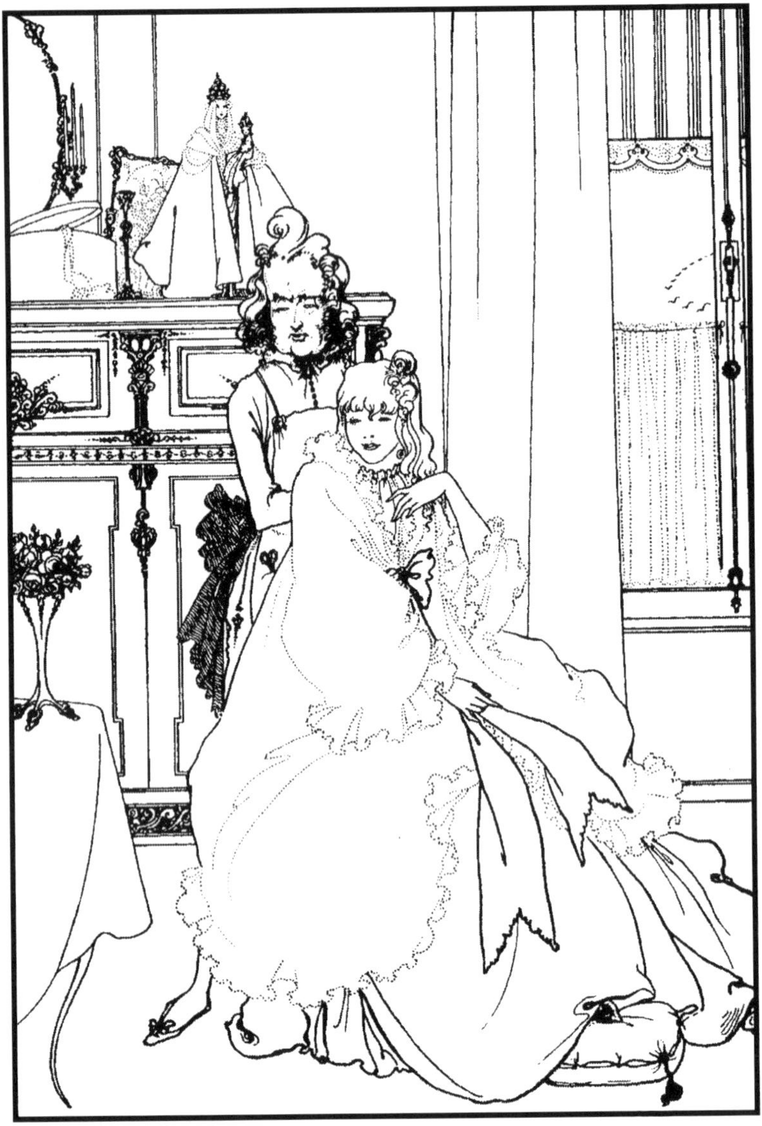

# Dad of the Year

"Since my mother wasn't around much as I was growing up, the task fell to my father to clue me in about becoming a woman. And with not more than a few sweat beads on his forehead, he gave me a reasonably straightforward, accurate, and non-threatening description of what was awaiting me. Unfortunately, he forgot to mention the emotional ride my hormones would take me on when they kicked into gear.

"The summer I was eleven, I was thrilled to be registered for tennis camp. I had visions of looking adorable in my tennis outfits and then jumping into the pool in my new swimsuit. It was the first summer I could debut my newly developed breasts, which should have been a clue to what was coming my way. But none of my friends had started their periods, and it was the farthest thing from my mind.

"When Dad came into my room the morning I was to leave for camp, he found me sobbing on my bed. I told him I couldn't go to camp because I started my period and I just couldn't let anyone know. He went straight to the store and bought me pads. In those days wearing one was not unlike straddling an outrigger canoe. When I wailed that I just couldn't wear those humongous things with my swimsuit, he disappeared into the kitchen with the pads. He returned with what may have been the very first mini-pads. He had cut each Kotex into three little pads so that I could wear them under my swimsuit and still keep my precious secret. Mother may not have appreciated what a sensitive man he was, but that eleven-year-old girl is forever grateful."

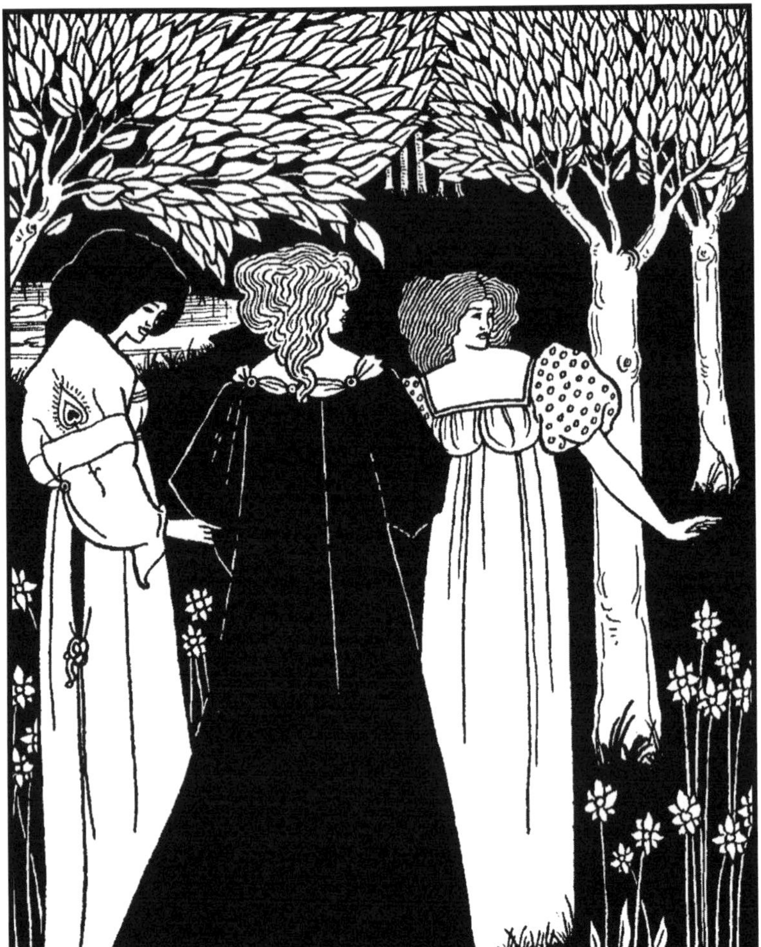

# Part Three

# Welcome to the Club

Every women remembers when and how she crossed that most daunting threshold into womanhood; how she heard about the facts of life; how she felt when she had her first flow; and last but not least, how she maneuvered her first tampon, if she had the nerve to try. Strong emotions create vivid memories. Menstruation is like childbirth and death in that, no matter how hard you bribe, plead, or cajole, you just can't get someone else to do it for you. Here now are women's stories of how each one faced this moment of truth.

# Urgent News

"Dad always wanted a son, but ended up with my older sister and me. He wasn't really disappointed though, because I turned out to be the world's biggest tomboy. While my sister stayed inside with Mom, learning how to bake cookies and sew on buttons, I was outside with Dad, learning how to bait a hook or tune a carburetor. When my sister was playing the piano, I would be up a tree. But as my puberty was approaching, I guess Mom realized I needed to be filled in on the necessary information about being female. I figure this must have hit her as an instant and urgent revelation because of the weird way she told me.

"I was playing catch with my father in the front yard one summer evening. My older sister came running out of the house and told me, 'Mom needs to talk to you, right now!' Thinking I was in trouble for something, I asked her what was wrong. My sister turned her palms up, shrugged, and said, 'She's in the bathroom.' As I walked into the house, scratching my head with my baseball mitt, I reviewed the list of my most recent crimes and tried to remember if any had gone unpunished so far. I couldn't think of any.

"When I knocked on the door, Mom told me to come in. She was in the middle of taking a bath, and told me to sit down on the toilet seat. She then proceeded to launch into an explanation about periods and pregnancy, most of which I had already gleaned from friends at school. To this day I cannot understand why it was so urgent that she tell me while she was taking a bath. Maybe she thought her lecture would be enhanced by visual aids. Maybe she couldn't find an anatomical chart illustrating breasts and pubic hair, so she decided to be the example. But being a woman of the fifties, the only place she could feel comfortable being naked was in the tub."

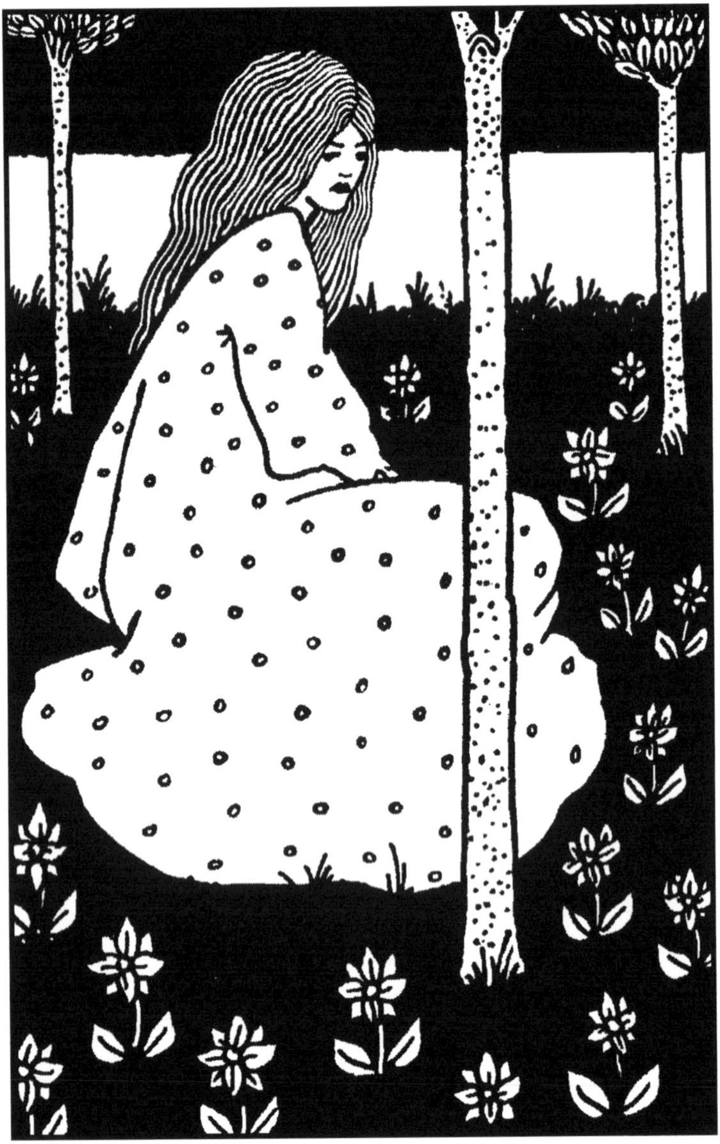

# Little Miss Literal

"My mother had a congenital heart condition, and it was really a miracle that she survived my birth. I worried about her constantly. When I was very young, I was certain that the quality of my behavior determined the state of her health. I would never step on cracks in the sidewalk or ever say the word 'die' out loud. I also took things too literally. When Dad went and donated at a blood drive in our school gym, I asked him why he was giving blood. He told me it was so the Red Cross could take it over to where men were fighting. After that, I always had a vision in my head of the school gymnasium, with people lying on cots donating blood at one end, and a boxing ring with boxers fighting at the other end. I had seen *Friday Night Fights* on television, and I knew that sometimes the men fighting got cut and lost blood.

"When Mother broke the news to me about menstruation, she explained it by saying that when a woman didn't get pregnant, she had some extra blood in her body that she didn't need for the baby, and for several days each month, her body got rid of the surplus. The only problem was that she neglected to mention where the blood exited exactly. For several years, I kept watching for this leaking blood around my fingernails and toenails and around my face and ears. When I finally did start my periods, Mother had died from the heart condition two months earlier. There was no one I trusted enough to talk about it. I was one sad young girl."

# Playing Hooky

"When I was nine, my mother sent away to the Kotex company for a free booklet called 'Now You Are Ten.' It came in a sealed wrapper, so I couldn't read what was inside when I brought in the mail the day it arrived. When Mom came home from work and put the booklet in her dresser without comment, I figured it was a surprise for my next birthday and promptly forgot about it.

"Some months later, I made the big mistake one day

of gossiping about a new girl in school whose family had just immigrated from Italy. Because she was not fluent in English, they put her back in the fourth grade, even though she was old enough for sixth grade. She loomed above the rest of us and quickly took control of the playground at recess. Although her father supposedly worked in an umbrella factory, I just knew he had to be in the Mafia. All I did to incur her wrath was comment to my friends that she cheated at tetherball. On the way home from school, a friend told me that Miss Mafia was going to pound me at recess the next day — pound being the fourth-grade term equivalent to pummel, punish, or pulverize.

"The next day, I concocted an imaginary stomachache so I could miss school for the first time ever in my grade school career — even though it meant forfeiting my perfect attendance certificate at the year-end assembly. Mom delayed going to work a little while and brought me a hot water bottle for my nonexistent stomachache. I had all but forgotten about the mysterious booklet until she pulled it out and began showing me its contents. I seem to recall some gory illustration of a side view of a woman's innards. The whole menstruation thing seemed so revolting that it actually did make me sick to my stomach and I threw up.

"I didn't start my periods until three years later. But when it did happen, I always got nauseated on the first day. I can't help but wonder if I subconsciously made a mental and physical connection between menstruation and nausea — a condition I lived with until I eventually had a hysterectomy. What a price to pay for one day of playing hooky. And by the way, I never did get that pounding. I just got called 'a big chicken,' which all things considered, was pretty accurate."

# What's for Lunch?

"My grandparents spent their summers on a private lake in California, and the highlight of my summer break was always the time I got to spend at their cottage. During the summer between my seventh and eighth grades, I was sent for two weeks at the lake. My grandparents had a leaky old row boat which I loved to take out at day break, but they didn't trust me on my own. One morning, I dragged Grandma out in the boat as soon as the sun was up and began rowing with a vengeance. Mid-lake, Grandma's eyes focused on my sprawled crotch. When I asked her what was wrong, she asked me if my mother had talked to me about women's cycles. When I told her we had a whole unit on puberty in health class, she pointed out the little splotch of blood that was spreading on the crotch of my pedal pushers.

"I rowed back to the cottage where Grandma gave me a Kotex and sent me to the bathroom. She told me to change the pad when it got soggy, and she warned me that the used pad would have a bad odor that would need to be wrapped in aluminum foil to contain the smell. So when my first pad started to have a water-logged feeling, I put on a fresh pad and took the used one to the kitchen to find the aluminum foil. I wrapped it in two layers to be extra sure it was secure and left it on the counter while I went to ask Grandma where to put it. Meanwhile, Grandpa came into the kitchen in search of some tasty leftovers that Grandma always kept from the dinner before.

"Without going into further detail, let me just say that when Grandpa unwrapped the foil package I had left on the kitchen counter, he totally lost his appetite."

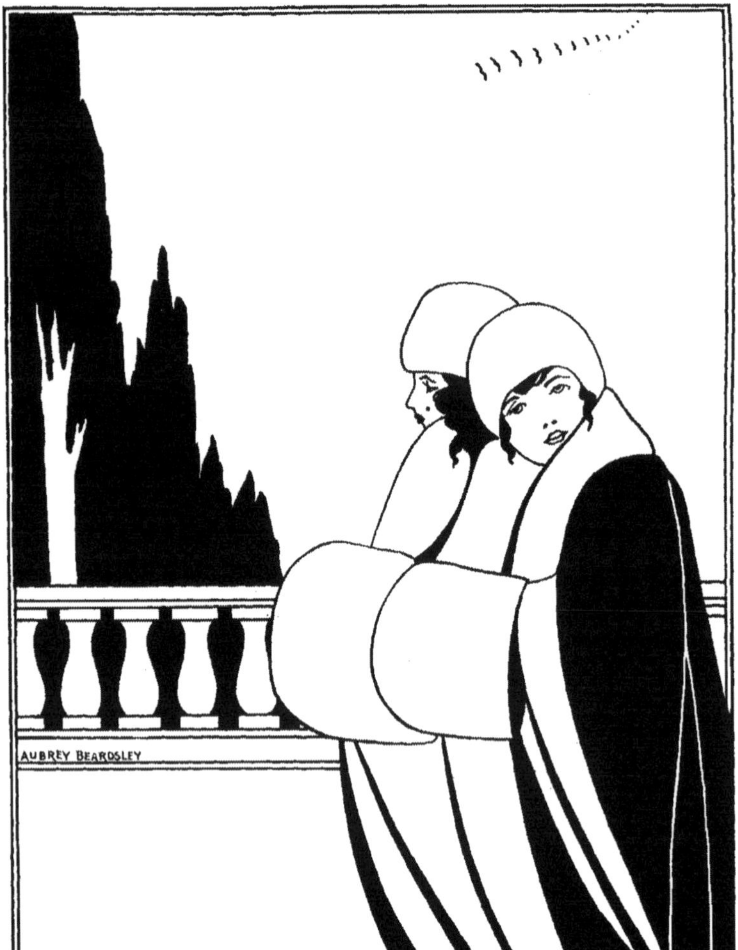
AUBREY BEARDSLEY

# Double Trouble

"When my identical twin sister and I first got the lecture about menstruation in health class, we weren't overly concerned about it. When the first of our friends started her period, we thought, 'Oh, poor thing!' Then when all of the rest of our friends had started their monthly cycles and we had not, we began to wonder if we were some kind of freaks of nature. Our mother assured us that all of the women in our family were 'late bloomers,' but we were at the age when 'mothers know nothing.' By age fourteen, all of our friends were sporting sanitary supplies in their backpacks, so my sister and I decided we might as well carry some pads and tampons, just in case. Month after month passed and when our supplies started looking pretty dog-eared, we would toss them out and replace them with fresh ones.

"At fifteen, we decided that we had really better be prepared and put sanitary pads in our undies every so often. This helped support the lie we had perpetuated to our friends that we had both started our periods. In fact, we told them we had started simultaneously, which they all thought was very cool. We even practiced inserting tampons, just to make certain we knew how when the time came. We had heard that using Vaseline would make it easier, which we have since found out is not a safe practice. We didn't have any Vaseline handy, so we used what we thought was the next best thing — Vicks Vaporub! We found out quickly that Vicks is not the petroleum jelly of choice.

*Welcome to the Club*

"We continued this pantomime of having periods together until we were sixteen. Then one day, the unthinkable happened. My sister started and I did not. Since we had told all our friends that we had begun years ago, she had no one to brag to except me. I assumed I would be starting any minute as well and kept checking my underwear every half hour. I installed a pad and kept Midol close at hand.

"Day after day passed, with still no long-awaited sign of womanhood. Three months went by, and I decided that I must be the victim of a genetic defect. I thought of how Siamese twins sometimes had only one organ between them, and they had to share that organ their entire lives. Maybe in the process of cell division, my sister and I were really meant to be Siamese twins. Maybe we accidentally got separated in the womb, and my sister ended up with the only uterus.

" I had resigned myself to being an anatomical anomaly, when one day at school, my pants felt damp. I signaled my sister, who was in class with me, to sit tight when the bell rang. When the room was empty, she checked out my rear and let out a squeal. We hugged and jumped up and down as if we had just made straight A's on our report cards. Of course, we couldn't tell anyone why we were so excited, and I realized that, ironically, I was totally unprepared that day. But, no matter, I knew just what to do, and I thanked God that night for not letting me be a side-show freak."

# Tampon Taboo

"The day I started my period, I reported directly to my mother, who handed me a box of maxi-pads without making eye contact and mumbled that I was never to use tampons. Now for several years, I had heard my friends complain about messy pads and rave about how cool it was to use tampons. So naturally, I wanted to be just like them. Normally, I would have whined and argued with my mother to get my way, but this was a subject about which Mother never spoke. For some reason, I was too intimidated to argue with her about internal vaginal devices, when she couldn't even broach subjects like diarrhea or constipation.

"I decided to just sneak tampons into my room and use them without her knowing. The problem was that I had to buy the tampons with my own money. My mother must have planted an ever-so-tiny seed of shame about the tampons though, because when I reached the drug store, I couldn't bring myself to pick up a package. I remembered all the times I had passed the feminine hygiene boxes in the grocery aisle as a little kid. I had asked Mom why the boxes never said what was inside. What was a Modess? What was a Tampax? Why were the boxes so boring looking? Mom had always told me to never mind, and the mystery boxes remained on the shelf. She had never bought sanitary supplies in my presence.

"When I found myself, money in hand, unable to lift the tampon box off the shelf, I went home defeated and used one of the maxi-pads that always would appear in my bathroom. After I went away to college, I thought I was up

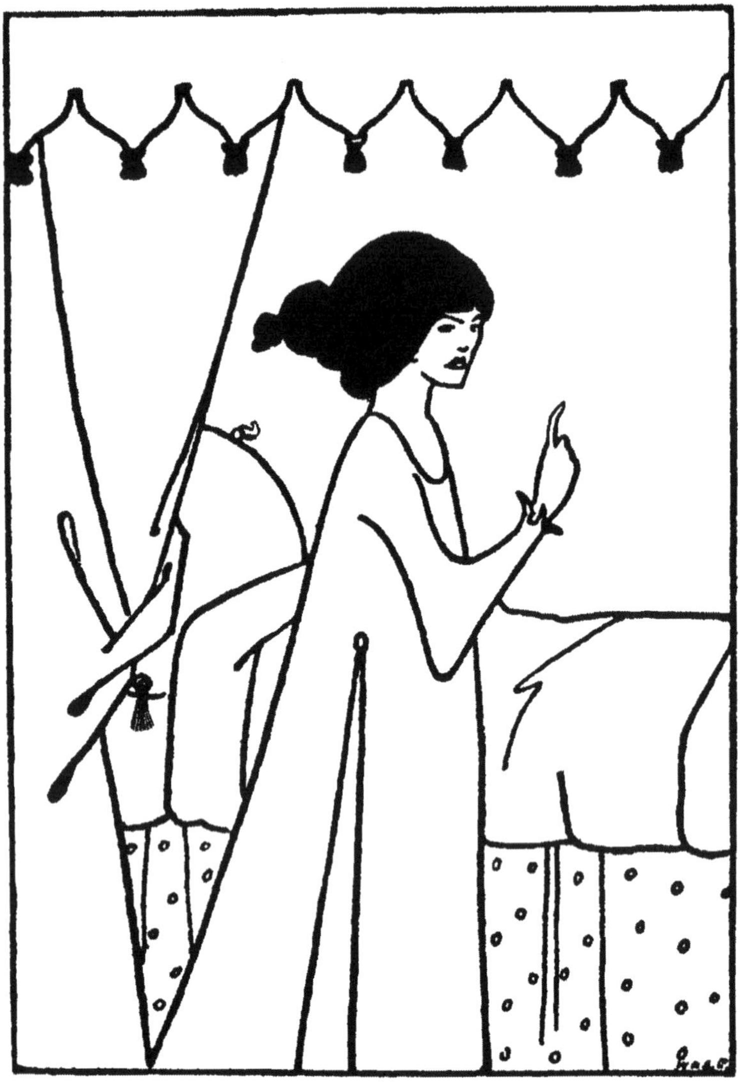

to the task. But when I went to the school store, half the football team was hanging around the checkout register, and I left empty handed. Next, I went to a busy grocery store and scoped out a female checker with no line. I grabbed a box of tampons and quickly went to her checkout counter. This was before the days of scanners and bar codes. Unfortunately, I had grabbed a box whose price sticker had fallen off, so the cashier had to call for a price check over the loudspeaker. 'Hey, Roy, can I get a price check on Tampax, regular size, forty-eight count?' When Roy came up to the counter with the price, I was horrified; I had not brought my purse and had no money. Totally flustered, I ran out of the store and retreated again to the maxi-pad box.

"For years after that, I would drive to stores outside of my neighborhood when I needed to buy tampons. I would stick them in my shopping cart underneath other items and wait until a woman checker was available. Even then, I would make small talk with her to try and distract her from the nature of my purchase.

"Luckily, my paranoia left me as soon as I had my first baby. Infants, with their dirty diapers and inevitable vomiting, force you to face aversions you never thought you could handle. Now I can throw tampons in the grocery cart along with ketchup or Preparation H. I realize I've come a long, long way, although I confess I'd still drive to another neighborhood if I had to buy lice shampoo. But tampons — no sweat."

# Puppy Love

"Probably the most embarrassing moment of my life happened when I was thirteen and my mom had just remarried. To help me through the transition, or maybe just as a bribe, my new stepdad bought me a golden Lab puppy. I named him Gumbo. One day when I was having my period, I wrapped up a soiled Kotex in toilet tissue and put it in the trash. While no one was watching, Gumbo dragged it out of the trash, marched proudly into the living room, and chewed it in front of my stepfather, who just sat there. I walked through the living room and saw the scene. I shooed Gumbo outside and then cleaned up the mess while my stepfather tried to ignore the whole thing.

"I never told Mom about what happened, but from then on, I was less than impressed with her choice of husband. He could have used that opportunity to be a real hero to me. That marriage only lasted eighteen months, but fortunately I got to keep the dog. Mom's next husband brought his cat when he moved in with us. That kept Gumbo sufficiently distracted that he never bothered my Kotex again. Mom made a much better choice in husband number three. In fact, that marriage is still going strong. Now, when I look at a man as a potential husband for me, I just ask myself if the guy in question would be the type to sit on the sofa and ignore the problem. If I can picture that old scene with him in my stepfather's place on the couch, I pass and keep looking."

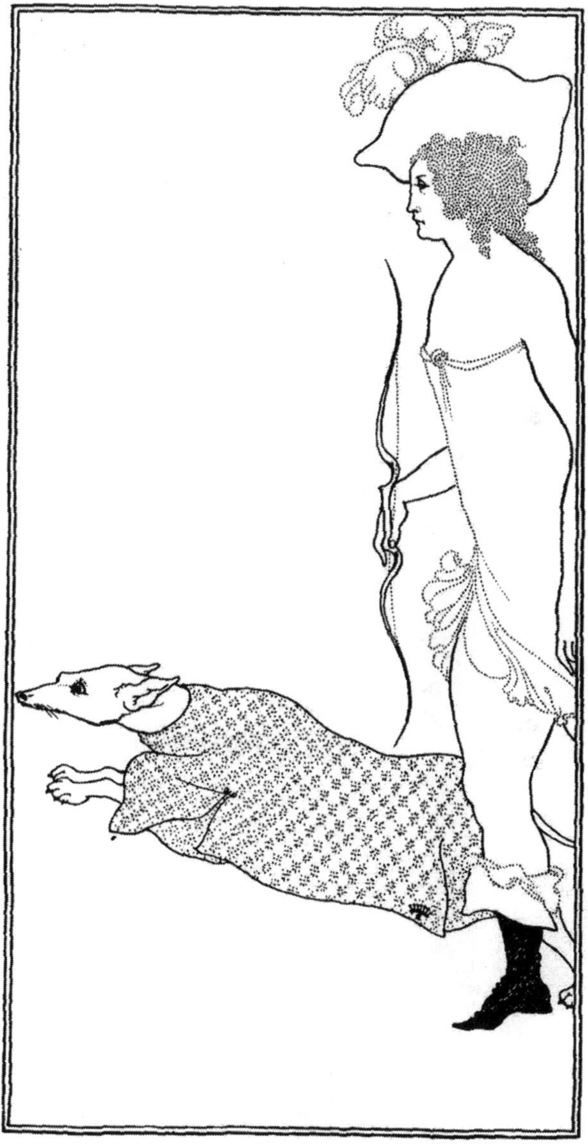

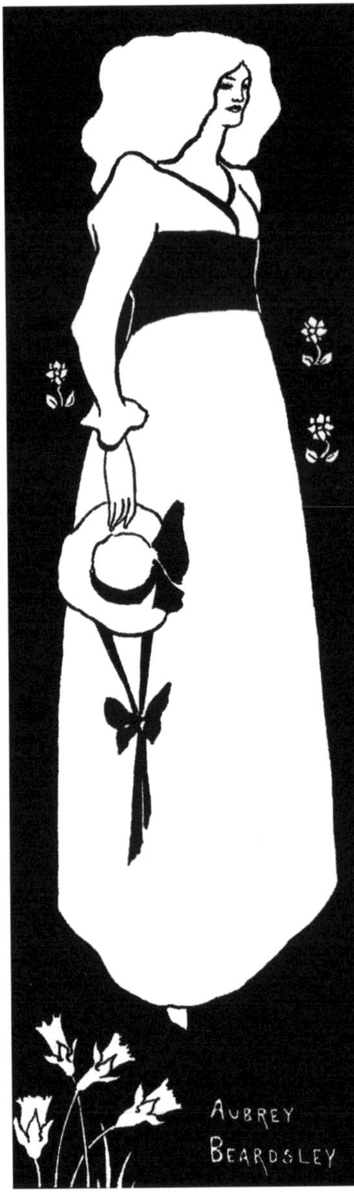
AUBREY
BEARDSLEY

# Two Rites of Passage

"My mother died when I was eleven, and one of the things she made me promise was to be confirmed in the Catholic church and take First Communion. Needless to say, I was not overly impressed with a God who would let a good person like my mother die, while criminals and other less worthy people still lived. But I faithfully, if not wholeheartedly, continued my catechism classes, hoping that my angel mother was looking down on me and was pleased.

"My grandfather bought me a beautiful white communion dress and veil, and I have to admit that I felt like something special was about to take place when I put it on. As I sat in the church pew waiting to take my First Communion, my first period came as well, ruining my white dress in the process. Maybe the onlookers thought it was a sign from above. Maybe they felt pity for me. After the mass, my Aunt Bessie took me to the bathroom and pinned up the back of my dress to hide the stains. She gave me hurried instructions about what was happening and said she had saved my mother's rag supply that I could use.

"For many years, I tried to figure out what I had done to deserve such punishment from God. First, He had taken my mother. Then, He had given me an obvious sign of displeasure by ruining my First Communion. I laid in bed at night, and when others were talking to God, I talked to my mother. I pictured her with beautiful strong wings hovering over me, listening attentively as I told her about my lonely life."

# On Your Toes

"I think the constant physical exertion of ballet dancing may have delayed my periods for a while — which was fine with me. When I finally did start at sixteen, it couldn't have been on a worse day. I was scheduled to audition to be accepted to the most prestigious student summer dance program in the country, sponsored by the American Ballet Theater. There was no way I could perform comfortably with a pad, so I had to tough it out and use a tampon on my very first day. I got accepted to the program, despite the fact that my focus was distracted from my pirouettes to my tampon.

"The timing of my periods continued to be inconvenient during my dancing career and often caused havoc for me. One night my dad was sitting proudly among the large audience during my performance. I was wearing a pink leotard and started my period on stage. Fighting panic, the moment I got off stage, I ran to the dressing room, inserted a tampon, ran cold water on the blood stain on my leotard, dried the wet spot with a blow dryer, and just barely made my next entrance. But there's more.

"The following incident, fueled by sheer desperation, quickly became a legend around the theater. I was performing in a flesh-colored leotard with no tights and started my flow in the middle of a performance. I didn't have enough time between entrances to change, so I commandeered a leotard from another dancer who had just come offstage and who had no more entrances. Unfortunately, this left my colleague standing nude in front of the stage hands. Luckily, she understood my plight and has been one of my closest friends ever since. I don't know anyone else who would have embarrassed herself to save me from being humiliated on stage like she did."

# Motel Hell

"It was a real treat for me to be invited for a weekend at a beach motel with a friend's family when I was about ten. The flea bag motel was in a cheesy seaside town with a few arcades. But it was my very first stay in a motel, so it could have been the Ritz for all I knew. Three of us girls got to share a double bed in our own room. And wouldn't you know the Fates would choose that night for my friend Susan to be initiated into womanhood? We woke up in those stark white cotton sheets to find that Susan had bled all over the bed as well as the three of us. We pulled off the bedding and crammed as much of it as we could into the tiny bathroom sink. We took the miniature bar of Dial soap and rubbed it into oblivion. But the blood had dried and looked pretty horrendous to the three of us under those harsh motel lights.

"Panic ensued when Susan's dad knocked on the door to tell us it was time to leave. We had no way to dry the sheets and couldn't figure out any way to hide them. We were certain there would be some terrible penalty for ruining sheets in a motel, like defacing school property or something. We decided the best course of action was to make the room as tidy as possible. So we took the stained and sopping sheets and made the bed, complete with the square corners we had learned to make in 4-H Club. Living 120 miles away, we figured it would be pretty tough for the motel owners to track us down if we got out fast.

"The next summer on a camping trip, I was relieved when I started my period in the privacy of my own sleeping bag."

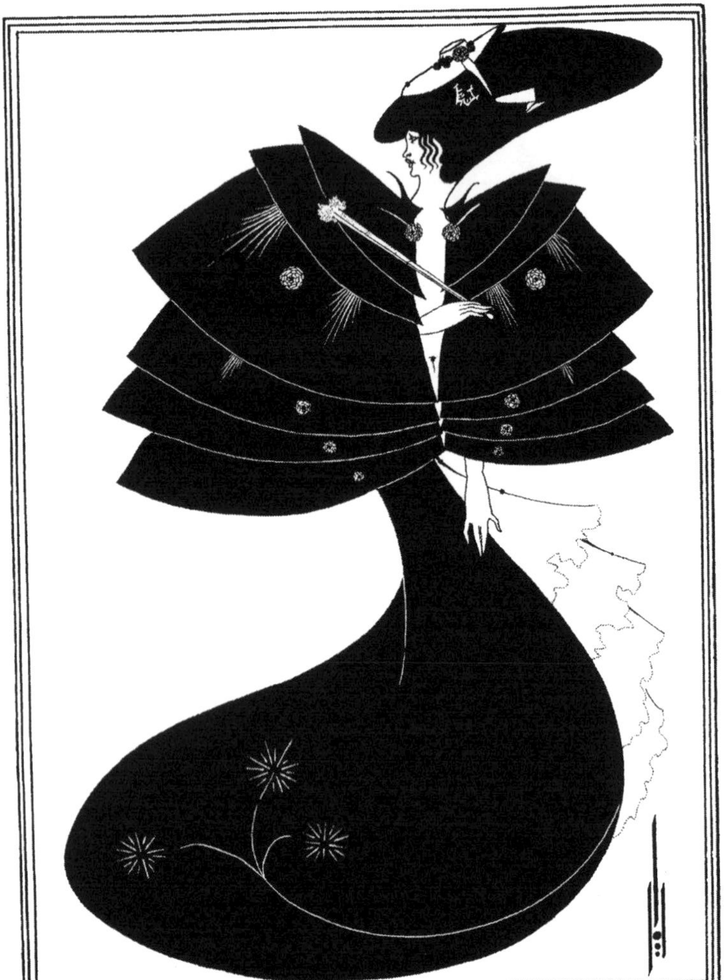

# Spotlight and Stage Fright

"Why does your first period start at the least convenient moment possible? As a new Freshman in high school, I thought I was really hot stuff when I somehow won a part in the school play as a New York snob who wore a slinky black dress. Imagine me, thrown in with veteran actors, some of whom actually had a driver's license! Two hours before the premier, I thought I was bleeding to death, until it occurred to me that it was my first period. The only supplies Mother had in the house were tampons, and asking her to explain their proper use to her teenage daughter would have been the equivalent of asking her to perform live sex on stage. It was bad enough having her baby girl prance on stage with a skin tight dress, but asking her to discuss the 'v' word was insanity.

"Well, we raided the cleaning closet and improvised with an ample supply of rags. Thus, I made my stage debut waddling with this mattress between my legs in my black dress, which now served more as a sausage casing. But something quite wonderful happened when I stepped out on stage. I was no longer the petrified rookie ninth grader. I was this sophisticated woman who also has periods, thank you very much. The play went splendidly, although I doubt that my mother ever saw my face or heard a word, with her eyes riveted as they were on my crotch!"

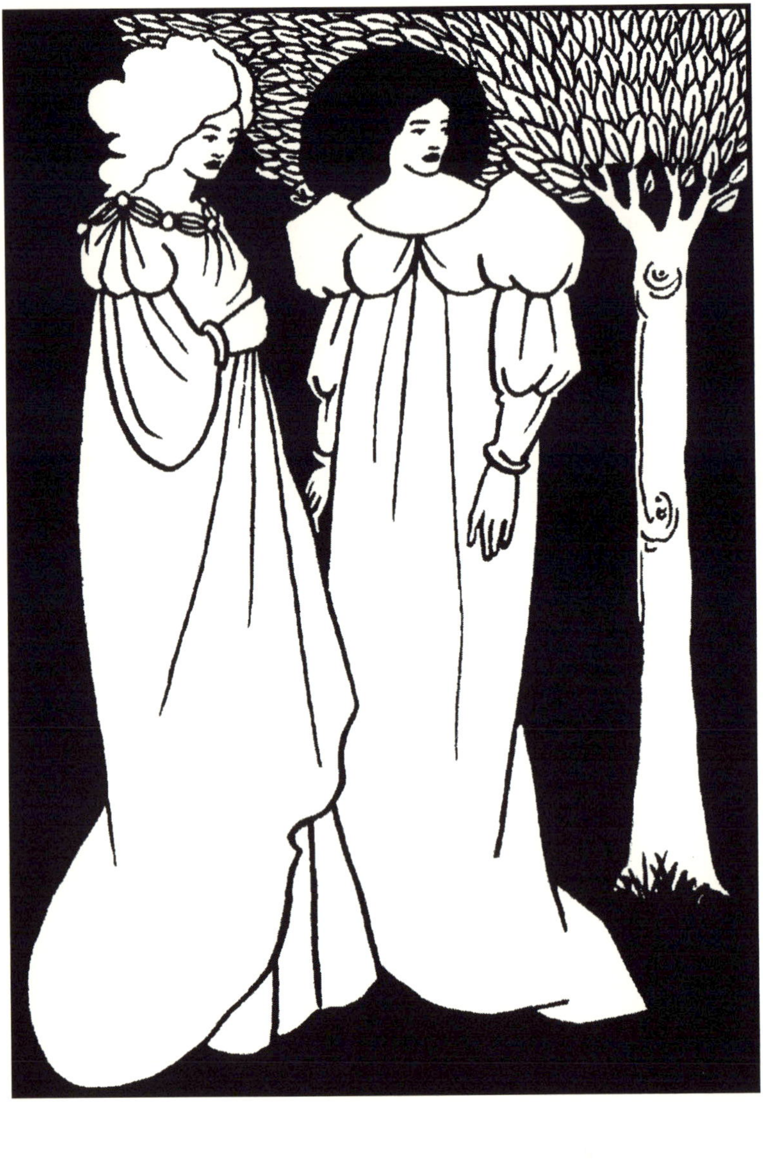

# Why White?

"On the day in junior high school that I chose to wear my brand new white pleated skirt, I rode the bus to school like every other day. As I walked off the bus, I felt a little funny. And then someone yelled at me, 'Hey, you must have sat in something. You've got something all over the back of your skirt.' I made my way to the office and called Mom. Fortunately, she came immediately and took me home for the rest of the day. She finally spilled the beans about the facts of life, seeing that I had already discovered some of it the hard way.

"Why do we always choose white on 'those days'? Is there a connection in our distant memory to some ancient temple priestess conducting sacred fertility rituals in a white gown? Or is it a divine trick to teach us forbearance and triumph over humiliation? Or is it those gorgeous models wearing white in the Tampax ads? Why aren't we attracted to black, the one color in which we could leak like a stuck pig and no one would be the wiser? No one has ever stood at the basin in agony, scrubbing furiously, trying to eradicate a persistent blood stain out of *black* undies. Before the days of Biz bleach, there wasn't much hope for the unfortunate white garment unwittingly chosen for sacrifice to the monthly cycle."

# Dilatation and Curettage

"I definitely think I deserve an award for having the most brutal introduction to the world of menstruation. At thirteen, I woke up confused one morning, thinking I had somehow wet the bed. Mortified, I threw back the covers and saw my bedding saturated in blood. I screamed hysterically at sufficient decibels to bring my father crashing through the door to rescue me from whatever was causing the ruckus. He took one look at his baby girl lying in a pool of blood and swept me and the bloody bedding into his arms and threw me in the car. He ignored every traffic light and speed limit to get me to the nearest hospital emergency room. His panic of course confirmed my own suspicions that I would die at any moment. The medical staff was perplexed at the profuse bleeding and eventually concluded that the best course of action was to perform a D and C. Now, although this is the same procedure used after childbirth and for abortions, I believe it is safe to assume that in those cases the woman is *not* a virgin. Consider, however, the plight of a thirteen-year-old who had never even been kissed, let alone have another human touch her nether regions.

"Before it was over, I began to wish that I really had died. For a while, I lived in terror of each monthly cycle, never knowing if my uterus would get cantankerous that month and send me back to the emergency room. But after a time, I actually got fairly blasé about waking up in a blood bath. The doctors could never figure out what caused the awesome hemorrhaging, so they just gave me a D and C whenever it happened. Ho, hum. But I still think I deserve some kind of award."

# Grace Period

"I got my first period on the day of Princess Grace's wedding. Years later, when my daughter was the same age I had been, I was listening to the radio at work and feeling nostalgic because the disk jockey announced that it was the anniversary of Princess Grace's wedding day. Just then, my daughter called from home to tell me she had started her period. Later that day we went out to dinner to celebrate the occasion and the wonderful synchronicity."

# Only in Hindsight

"This incident was certainly not funny at the time, but the memory of it touches me terribly now. I grew up in the fifties in a family that was typically reserved and modest about everything having to do with the body. Soon after I started menstruating, I wanted to try tampons, but my mom had never used them, even though they had been available for twenty years. There I was, locked in the bathroom, frustrated and embarrassed while, outside the door, Mom coached me by shouting things like 'It's in the middle somewhere!' When I emerged triumphant from the bathroom, she applauded me for achieving what she hadn't brought herself to do. I felt so unencumbered and free. I walked around saying 'This is so exciting! This is so exciting!' We celebrated with what I consider to be the all-American tradition. We went out together for ice cream."

# Too Frugal

"Years of financial struggle made my mother tight with a dollar. She knew every possible way to stretch her meager weekly household allowance. We drank powdered milk. We ate liver and kidneys because they were cheap and most people considered them scraps for the cat. We drank Kool-Aid instead of expensive soda pop. She cleaned the windows with ammonia and newspapers instead of costly paper towels and Windex. We took our own popcorn to drive-in movies. And when I started my menstrual cycle, I found out about another way my mother saved money. She kept a package of Red Cross cotton in the bathroom and told me to just tear off a piece and put it in my panties whenever I was flowing. I didn't realize, until I talked to my friends, that I was the only girl using hunks of cotton. Desperately not wanting to be different, I spent my own allowance on genuine Kotex. Mother thought that was the height of extravagance and made sure that I at least used the coupons she clipped for me."

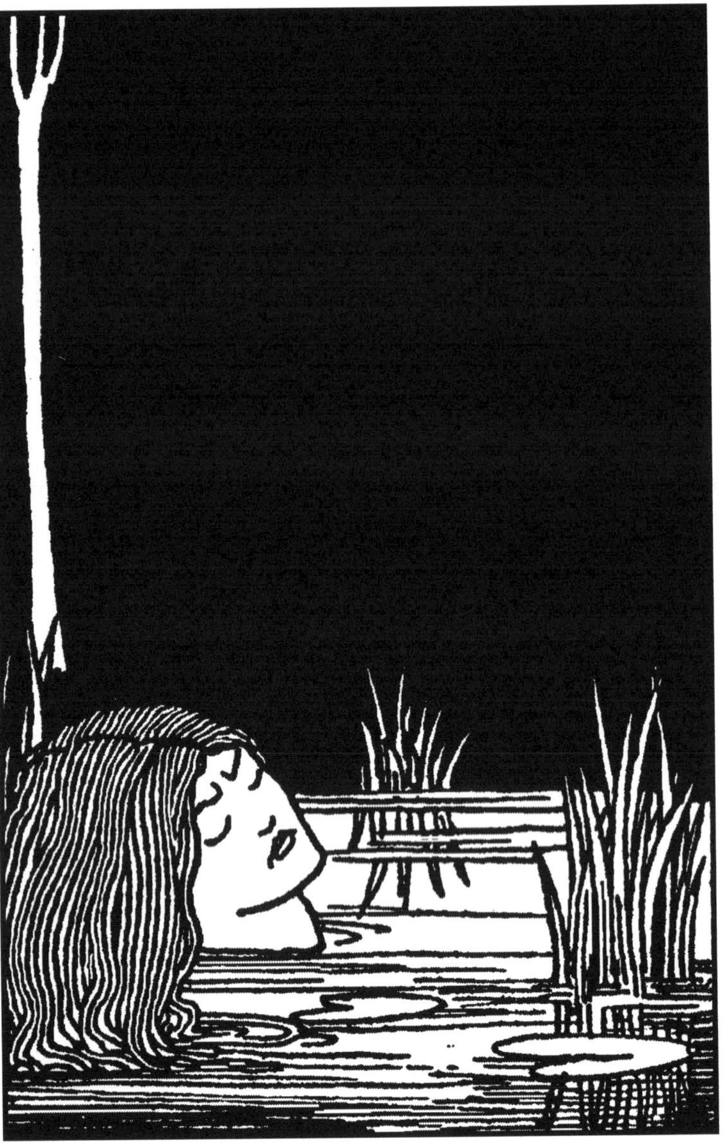

# Sink or Swim

"My eighth grade class celebrated graduation with a picnic and swimming party. I was so determined not to miss the event when I started my period that morning, that I told Mother I wanted to try a tampon. Being from the old school, she couldn't bring herself to tell me how, so she told me to ask my older sister. Unfortunately, I was afraid of my big sister because she was so weird. (She has since been diagnosed with bipolar disorder, but for many years we didn't understand what was wrong with her.) I always kept my distance from my sister, never knowing what would set her off on a rampage. She was mean enough that I could imagine her purposely telling me to do something that would actually hurt me.

"Taking everything into consideration, I decided to try and wing it with the tampon. So off I went to the picnic with my swimsuit, beach towel, and tampon. In the changing room at the pool, I took off the paper wrapper and didn't realize the cardboard was an applicator. I guessed it was to keep the tampon from getting crushed in storage, and I wondered what the string was for. I just laid the tampon lengthwise in the crotch of my swimsuit and figured I was all set. I went outside to the pool and jumped in. The tampon started swelling as soon as I was in the water, and I felt like I was swimming with a pillow between my legs. It occurred to me that I didn't really understand the tampon concept, so when I got home, I looked in the box to see if instructions were included. Sure enough, there they were, complete with illustrations. Aha! So they were worn internally. Imagine that!"

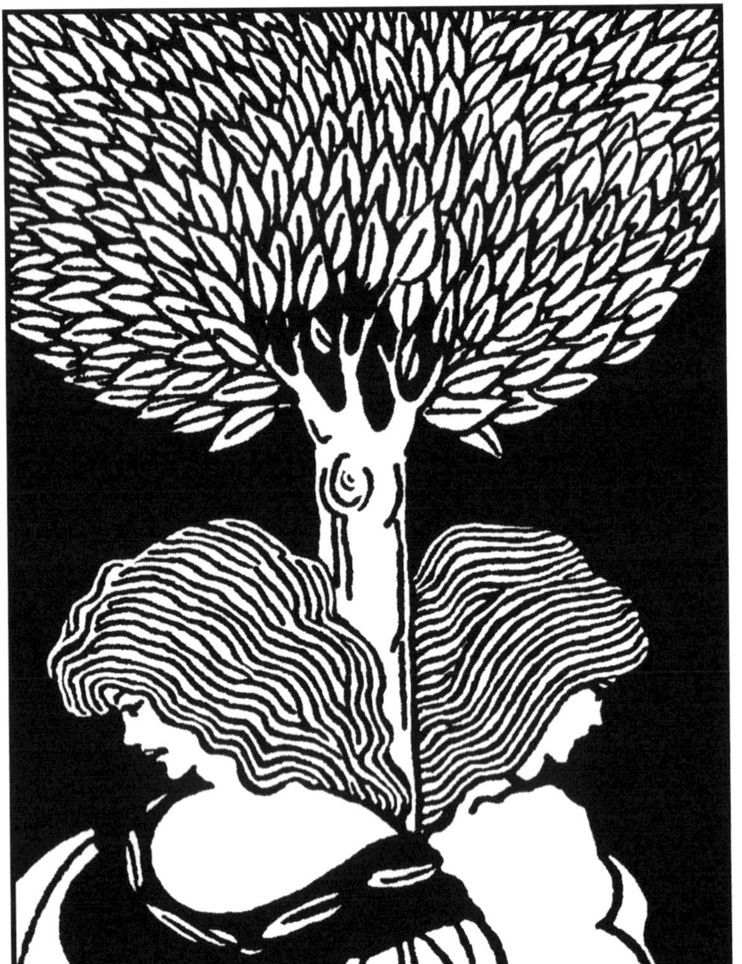

# My Shadow

"Now that I'm sixteen, I can look back and laugh about the first time I used a tampon. But when it happened back in junior high school, it wasn't funny. I was wearing this totally cute pair of GAP shorts in math class, and the teacher was talking about some bogus fraction thing. I guess I didn't have the tampon in exactly right because I could tell I was sitting on a huge problem. My best friend Ali was sitting by me, so I wrote her a note that said 'I'm leaking.' The teacher saw me hand her the note and came and grabbed it from her. How rude! He read the note and asked me if I would like to be excused. So I'm like all embarrassed and just shook my head no. My face felt hot and I probably looked totally stupid. Anyway, when class was over, Ali and I waited until everybody left the room. Then she stood right behind me and walked step-by-step with me to the office so nobody could see my butt. We kind of looked like these old movie guys called the Marx Brothers. I called Mom from the office and told her about my problem and which pair of shorts to bring me. Ali stayed right behind me all the way to the bathroom where I could change. And she stayed outside the stall while I tried to use a tampon properly this time. She would have been my best friend for life except her dad got transferred to Colorado. Sometimes I still e-mail her though. And we got in the same AOL chat room together one time, which was pretty cool — LOL."

# Cheerleaders

"After the big commotion about toxic shock syndrome, my mother levied a rule that there were to be no tampons in the house. My older sister tried to explain to her that toxic shock syndrome was related to super absorbent rayon tampons, which had been pulled off the market. As long as you used the regular cotton tampons, there was little risk. But Mother would have none of it. So when I started my period, there was never any chance for me to use a tampon. Consequently, I eventually ended up in a college dormitory being the only co-ed who had never taken the plunge. This fact came to light one night when I was playing a game of 'I Never' with some of my girlfriends. To play the game, people take turns saying something they have never done before. 'I never have tasted an oyster.' 'I never have tried pot.' 'I never have wet the bed.' Then the other players have to say whether or not they have done the thing named. When my turn came, it just slipped out, 'I never have used a tampon.'

"As the room was polled one by one, every other girl said she used tampons all the time. Taking pity on me, my friends abandoned the game, ushered me into the dormitory bathroom, handed me a tampon, and sent me into a stall. Everyone stood on chairs outside the stall, and each took turns offering her own special tips. One girl read aloud the tiny printed instructions in the box. One offered to put it in for me the first time. Another gave me a Q-Tip to test drive before using the bigger tampon. My cheerleaders hung like monkeys over my stall and never lost their enthusiasm for the task at hand.

"I tried several times with no success and was starting to fear that maybe I was built differently somehow. I realized I was feeling queasy and lightheaded from fear and frustration. A cold sweat broke out on my forehead. The whole room broke out in cheers when I finally emerged triumphantly. Of course, I wasn't actually having my period, but I decided to wear the tampon for a while — just to get the hang of it. There's not a month that goes by when I don't think about those friends and how bizarre they looked as I stared up at them from my seat on the toilet. How pitiful I must have looked to them as I tried to cross that daunting threshold to become a really modern woman."

*Welcome to the Club*

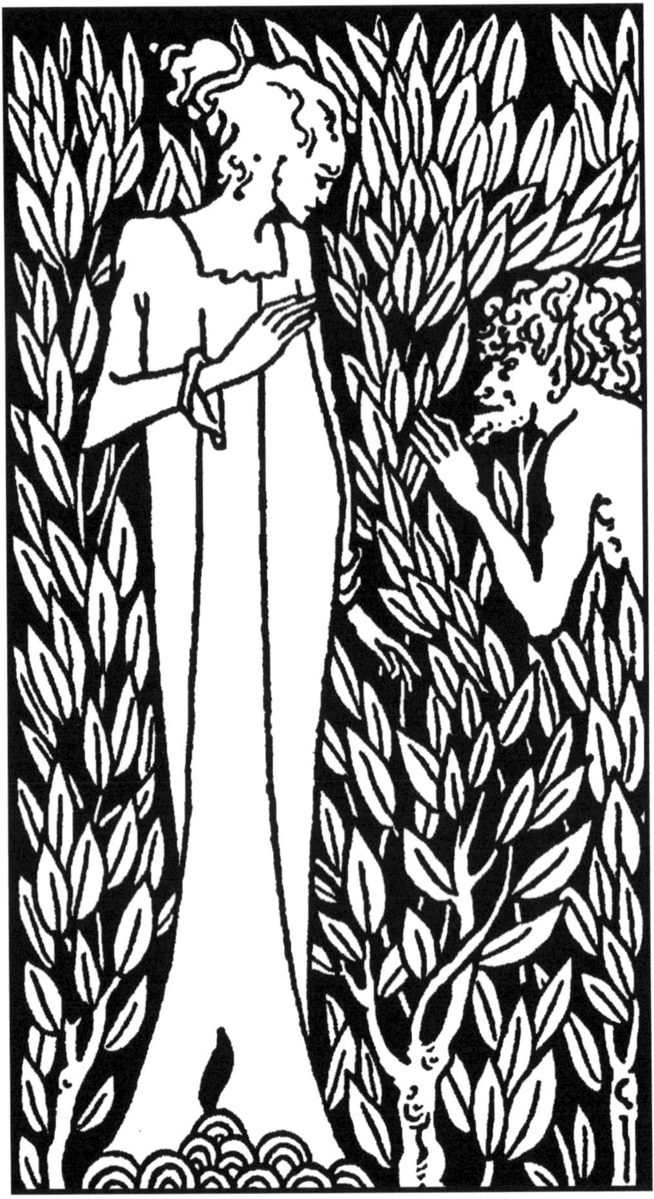

# Part Four
# The Crone Zone

The post-menopausal woman is considered the wise woman in matriarchal cultures. Technology has given new options to today's crone, who can forestall a dowager's hump and hairy chin with calcium supplements and synthetic hormones, who can reclaim her youthful color from a bottle of hair dye, and who can lipo-suck-and-tummy-tuck her way back toward her girlish figure. Today it takes a great many years to become an old woman, with "middle age" lasting well into the twilight years. A generation of women who have outlived their uteruses speak of their own experiences and how they contrast to the young girls of today.

# Coming into Heat

"I was born on a ranch in 1912, and I knew at an early age about animals coming into heat and mating. But it never occurred to me that human beings were subject to any sort of similar cycle. I was the eldest of six children, and although I had three sisters, Mother never spoke a word about menstruation, nor was it ever mentioned in school. Sex education would have sent the town elders into apoplexy. So when one day, at age sixteen, I began to have bleeding between my legs, it didn't dawn on me that this was no different than when the cows or horses were in heat. I thought I had a terrible disease in my bladder, and I just knew something that serious must be fatal. Mother had such a heavy burden on her shoulders, living in the rural countryside and raising six children, that I decided I could not add to her troubles by breaking the news that her sixteen-year-old daughter would soon be dead. I found some frayed old linens that I used like wound dressings and burned the used ones in the wood stove to hide the evidence. When the bleeding stopped after four days, I hoped maybe there was some chance for recovery. But when the problem returned a few weeks later, I knew I was doomed. I went on this way until the linen supply got so low that Mother questioned me about it.

"I broke into tears and confessed, desperately needing the comfort that only a mother's arms can provide. When Mother explained what was happening to me, I couldn't understand why she hadn't told me about it before, and I was angry. But of course now I realize that, if menstruation was such a closed subject during my childhood, it must have been even worse when she was a girl. I swore that when I had a daughter, I would show her the kindness of talking about it before she went through my ordeal. My own daughter only lived to age four, but I know that girls these days get a thorough explanation of their body functions in grade school. It would be nice if it came from their parents first, but at least the schools make sure the girls don't have to go through the secret fear and trauma I did."

# Surf's Up

"I may be a grandmother now, but back in the sixties I was one of the new breed — the California surfer girls — who were an inspiration to the Beach Boys, who I guess must be grandfathers themselves today. Groovy chick that I was,

I wouldn't have been caught dead in a one-piece swimsuit. Nothing but a bikini for this Gidget. This created a problem during my periods because there was no way I was going to stay on the beach when the surf was up. And being, during those years, under the influence of Doris Day and Sandra Dee, my role models, I was a virgin. Of course everyone knew that a virgin could not use a tampon and still remain a virgin. The only other option was to use that clumsy Kotex with its elastic sanitary belt. I had a bikini that actually exposed my navel, and there was no way to keep even a narrow belt hidden and tucked in a bikini bottom.

"One day, I made the unfortunate decision to just use a Kotex with no belt. As I walked to the water, I kept checking behind me to make sure there wasn't a white tail wagging in the breeze. Once you're in the water, the surf doesn't let you think about anything else. You focus on the wave patterns, get in position for the right wave, paddle like mad to catch it, stand up on your board when it catches you, work with it through your feet, and just enjoy. But in a calm moment between a set of waves, I realized that I couldn't feel the Kotex. Still on my board, I laid on my stomach so I could check around a little more discreetly, and sure enough, no Kotex. A big wave must have sucked that pad right off me and into the ocean. I just hope it didn't wash back onto the shore or choke a tuna.

"I was glad to discover that the bleeding stops in the water. It would have been nice if someone had told me beforehand. I spread the word to my friends so they wouldn't run into the same problem. But of course, some of them didn't worry about it anyway because they were those easy tampon girls."

# Groovin' Grandma

"As a grandmother of teenage girls, I chuckle when I think about the day I started my period at age twelve. I was raised by my father who took my sister and me to our grandparent's house while he worked. We were never told about menstruation, but Dad kept on saying something about one day we would change from a girl to a woman, with no other explanation.

"I was puzzled when I started my period at my grandparent's house, so I called in my ten year old sister for a consultation. We did in fact conclude that I was indeed now a woman, whereupon my sister began to cry because she thought I wouldn't be allowed to play with her anymore. When she calmed down, we conspired to conceal the situation from our grandparents.

"When Dad came to pick us up, we broke the news to him and asked if I would be having a baby now, because I really wasn't ready. He realized he couldn't put off the facts-of-life talk any longer, so he explained it as best he could, using such technical terms as 'thingamajig' and 'dealeebob.' I was glad to find out that I wouldn't be having a baby immanently, but was upset to find out that I couldn't go swimming when it was 'my time.' I told him not to tell Grandma and Grandpa because I just didn't think people of their age should be exposed to such information. But I knew it was no coincidence that a box of Kotex showed up the next day at their house.

"It's hard for children to imagine that their grandparents were ever young. So I make sure I talk with my granddaughters about bodies, periods, sex, and the whole kit and caboodle. They tell me I'm hip. I tell them they're the bees knees, and they say, 'whatever.'"

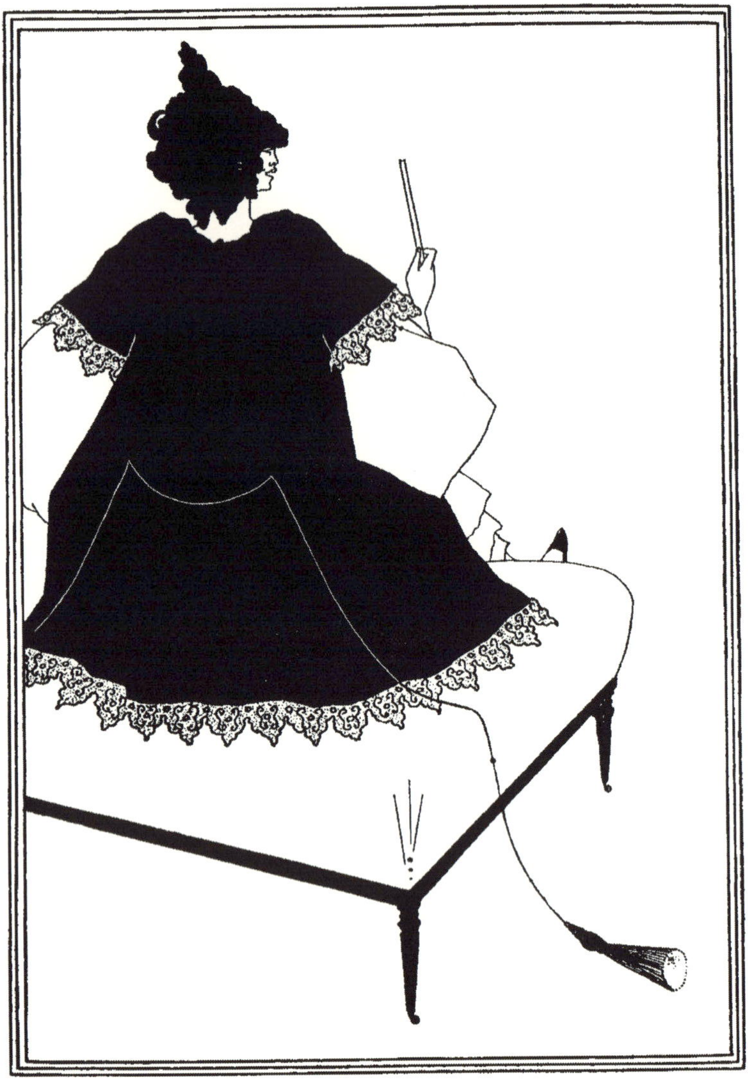

# New-Fangled Contraption

"My thirteen-year-old granddaughter came to visit me last summer, and wouldn't you know, she started her very first period at my house. She wasn't feeling very well, so I told her to rest while I went to the grocery store to get her some supplies. I kept going up and down the feminine hygiene aisle, but I couldn't find any sanitary belts. I figured they must be sold out, so I went next door to the pharmacy. Again, I couldn't find a belt. I finally asked a woman clerk where they kept the sanitary belts. You could tell that she thought a woman my age shouldn't be worrying about something like that. When I told her it was for my granddaughter, she laughed and told me that belts hadn't been worn for years and years.

"Good riddance I thought. I told her it had been thirty-five years since I had needed sanitary supplies, and she told me the paraphernalia had changed quite a bit in that time. Of course, she wasn't even thirty-five years old, so I must have been a talking history book to her. She gave me an education on the new pads, with their wings and adhesive strips and absorbency layers. I bought my granddaughter a nice selection for moderate and light days as well as protection for overnight. I couldn't help but compare them to the rags that I had to wash out when I was a teenager. Modern is much better."

# Achtung, Herr Doktor!

"My maternal grandmother was born in 1869 in a small village in southeast Germany. At the tender age of eighteen, she married the boy next door, with whom she had grown up. The young couple moved to a little town, not far from their birthplace and not a heck of a lot bigger. Rosa helped her husband, Herman, in his modest business, kept house, and raised five children. She was blessed with a strong back and good health, and the only time she came in contact with a physician was on the rare occasion when one of her children was seriously ill. In those days, common childhood ailments were cured with home remedies, and mothers never thought of consulting a physician, unless they were on their deathbed.

"When my grandparents' children were grown and on their own, the folks sold their business and moved to the big city where the kids had settled. Grandma did not care much for Berlin, kept to her modest and simple ways, and remained totally unimpressed with big-city sophistication on parade.

"Grandma Rosa was barely in her sixties when she confessed to her oldest daughter, my mother, that she was experiencing some rather unusual (for her age) 'female' problems. It took all of my mother's persuasive powers to convince her to see a gynecologist. Mother made the appointment with the doctor she had known for years, accompanied Grandmother to his office, handed her quickly over to the nurse before Grandma could change her mind, and took a seat in the waiting room.

"Less than thirty minutes later, the nurse told Mother the doctor wanted to see her in his private office. Doctor L. greeted her with a big grin on his face and told her about his encounter with Grandmother.

"The internal examination was a totally new and most disturbing experience for this simple country woman. Apparently, she had never even heard of such a thing before. Flat on her back, with her legs in those awful stirrups, she was covered with a sheet against the goings on as the doctor began his probing. It wasn't long before my little grandmother raised herself on her elbows and addressed the white tent in front of her in all earnestness, with the following words:

"'Young man, listen to me! Can you hear me, young man? Does your mother know what you are doing?'"

# Seiri-yo No

"My granddaughter, Jamie, was fortunate enough to go to Japan as a foreign exchange student at age thirteen. She lives with my divorced son, and before her departure, we had a big powwow about menstruation — just in case she started her gekkei (period) while she was on her trip. We packed her off with an ample supply of *seiri-yo no* (Kotex). It turned out that she didn't need them after all, but she was well prepared.

"When the daughter of Jamie's host family came in return to the United States, my son asked if the girls could both stay at my home. I was thrilled to have an international guest, especially over the Easter weekend. Although she couldn't speak much English, we had a great time as she demonstrated the art of using chopsticks and taught me to pronounce her name correctly.

"Eventually, I went to bed as the girls played some popular music — a common language for teens all over the world.

"About four o'clock in the morning, Jamie woke me up to tell me that our guest urgently needed my help. I went into the room to find her in tears, clutching a pillow to her stomach. Thinking my American cooking may have given her a stomachache, I raided my medicine cabinet for Pepto-Bismol, Mylanta, Tums, and Alka-Seltzer. She seemed hesitant to take any of them. Not only could I not understand the Japanese girl, but I didn't understand my granddaughter when I thought she asked, 'Don't you have any *tees?*' I asked her whether she meant golf tees or T-shirts. I couldn't imagine what medicinal value either one would have. She looked at me incredulously and said, 'Nooooo. You know, like green *teas* or black *teas*.'

"The nickel dropped when I recalled how I used to always crave tea when I had menstrual cramps. When I committed the *faux pas* of blurting out 'Is she menstruating?' both girls rolled their eyes up and turned identical shades of pink. Bearing in mind that it was four o'clock on Easter morning and that I hadn't had any sanitary supplies in the house since sometime during the Nixon administration, I set about trying to find something for her to use until the stores opened. I ended up offering her a flour sack and some safety pins. Our Japanese guest kept a stiff upper lip as she accepted the supplies and watched as I pantomimed how to use them. She disappeared into the bathroom, and I finally went to bed after she reemerged and politely bowed her thanks — all the while dying inside, I'm sure.

"As I climbed into bed, I noticed my 'bed buddy' — a horseshoe-shaped pillow that I heat in the microwave and wrap around my neck when it is stiff or sore. It dawned on me that the heat might feel great on her stomach, so I warmed it up for her. When I walked into the room and motioned with it toward her stomach, a look of sheer terror came over her face and she pulled the covers over her head. I realized that she thought I wanted her to use the monstrosity as a sanitary pad. I laughed and held the pillow to me like you might do to a stuffed animal. She got the idea and was most grateful as she cuddled it to her tummy.

"I gave up trying to sleep at six o'clock in the morning and went to the grocery store to get an update on the new generation of feminine hygiene products. I grabbed a couple of big milk chocolate Easter bunnies for good measure. No need for the memory of her first period to be a total downer — and I was certain that the craving for chocolate must be a part of the international sisterhood."

# Old Dog, New Trick

"When my husband and I retired, we started taking classes at the local community college. One of the classes was called Life Drawing. I had no idea what that meant until we walked into class with our new charcoal pencils and drawing tablets. On a revolving platform in the middle of the room was an artist's model taking off her robe. She had nothing underneath but her birthday suit. Well, almost nothing. Now, I could handle the nudity. After all, I may be old but I'm a modern thinker. And I could even handle it when she sat down on a low stool and exposed a dangling tampon string. But the thing I couldn't handle was, when I looked at my husband's sketch of her at the end of class, the old coot had drawn the woman, string and all. I withdrew us from the class and signed us up for Beginning Bonsai."

*The Crone Zone*

# The Mother of All Excuses

"I learned at a very young age that my monthly cycle was a great excuse in a wide variety of situations. When I was in junior high school, we had to wear a stupid uniform for gym classes, consisting of a white cotton short-sleeve shirt that was impossible to iron and a pair of navy blue twill shorts with leg openings so big you almost set sail on windy days. PE was my favorite subject, but I dreaded having to take communal showers with the other girls, who hated it as much as I did. The teacher stood at the shower room exit and checked off your name as you came out the door. If you tried to dash in and out too quickly, she blew her whistle and made you go back in again. Every girl felt humiliated being naked in public. The ones who hadn't developed felt guilty and worried about being immature. The ones who had developed felt embarrassed when the other girls stared at their new equipment. And of course you had to check out everyone else without being conspicuous, just to see how you compared.

"But having your period eased the situation a little

because, when you stood in line for attendance at the beginning of class, you informed the teacher that you would be having a 'half bath.' This entitled you to enter the edge of the shower in your shorts. But if you didn't take off your bra, the teacher threatened to cut it off with scissors. You had to dampen a towel and 'sponge' any exposed skin. As you checked out of the shower, you would get full credit for a shower that day. Ultimately, your PE grade was primarily based on how consistently you took your showers, which I suppose was as valid a criterion as any other.

"As I grew older, having my period continued to provide other great excuses. Like 'Not tonight, honey' or 'Could you take the kids swimming, dear?' or 'Could you do the grocery shopping? It's my time.' Over the years, I kept on thinking this would wear thin. But then I realized that a man has absolutely no idea what it is like, and I had it ingrained in my husband early on that bleeding each month was a pretty monumental thing. He even got in the habit of making certain I had stopped flowing before asking me to perform high risk activities like fishing or bowling.

"Now that I'm retired, I spend lots of time on the golf course with the gals. Every time I slice the ball, flub a sand shot, or yank a putt, I still blame it on my period. But I finally was called on the carpet by a golfing buddy of many years. She said, 'Knock it off. You haven't had a period in fifteen years.' I said, 'Shhhh! Don't let it get around.'

"One of these days, I guess I'll have to have to stop using my uterus as an excuse, or my friends will want to submit me to the *Guinness Book of World Records* as the oldest ovulating woman in history. And they're surely wondering why the box of Tampax in my bathroom is so dusty and faded.

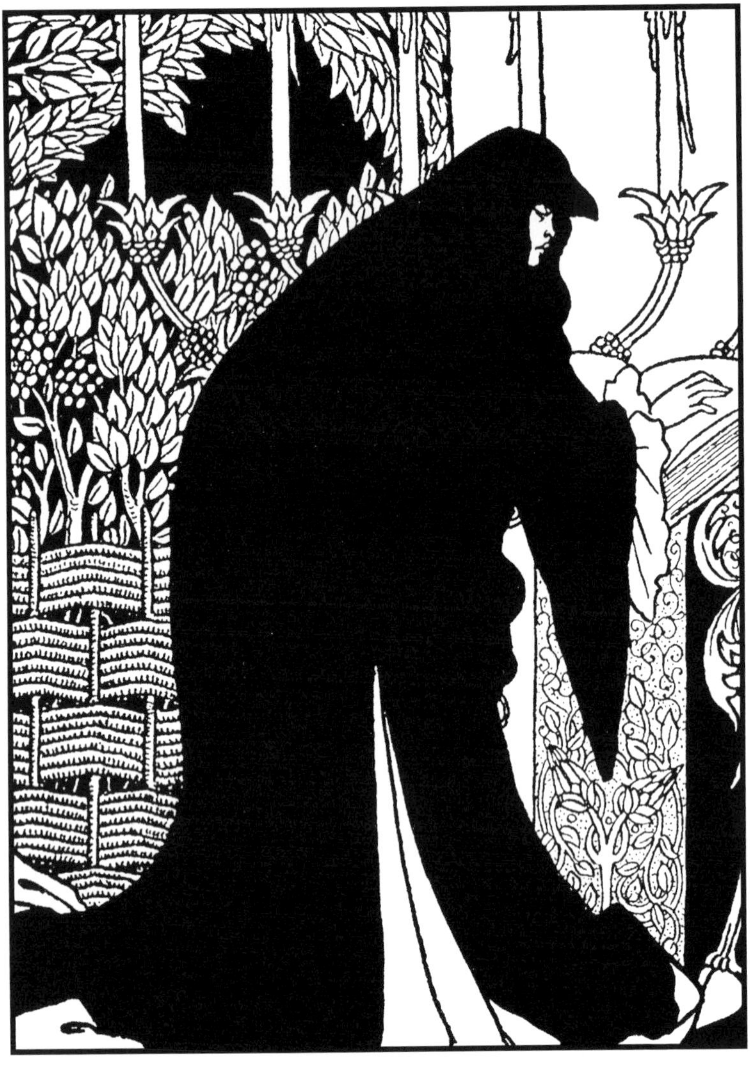

# Old Faithful

"When I turned forty, my kids were almost grown and I started thinking sadly about menopause. It's not that I wanted more kids, but there was something lamentable about not being able to if I wanted. I tried to be optimistic and prepare myself for the changes I thought would soon be taking place. When I turned fifty, I was tired of having periods and started getting excited about the freedom that would soon be mine. But when I turned sixty and my uterus kept chugging away every month like clockwork, I thought, 'enough is enough.' I made an appointment with my gynecologist and told him I wanted a hysterectomy. He said he would schedule me for a D and C procedure which was not as extreme and would make the flow less heavy. As they put me under anesthesia, my last words were, 'Feel free to take the whole uterus if you need to.' But when I woke up from my stupor afterward, I asked the nurse, 'They didn't do a hysterectomy, did they?' Damn. Old Faithful was still intact.

"I consider it a great biological injustice that I have to spend my Social Security checks on tampons. But I figured out a plan of action. I began a campaign of phone calls and appointments with my gynecologist complaining about uterine cramping. He's finally tired of my whining and has scheduled a hysterectomy for me in six weeks. Maybe it's unethical, but after fifty-five years of menstruation, I think I have earned a hall pass. And the idea of turning seventy and having to take Tampax to the senior center is discouraging. I've made my contribution to the gene pool and it's long past time for my uterus to take a well-deserved rest."

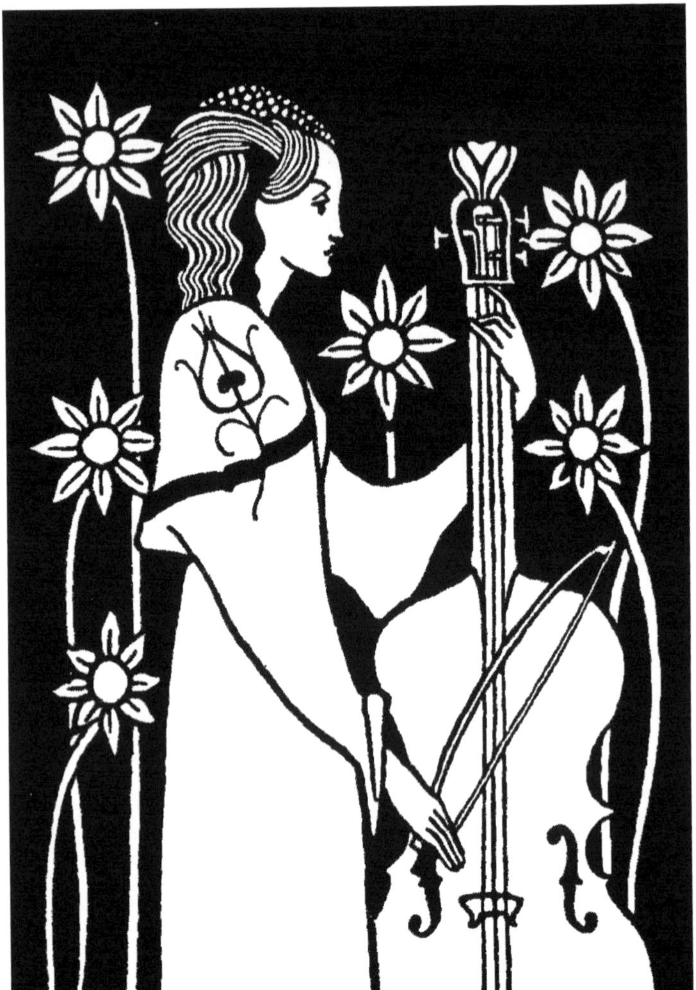

# Part Five

# Feeling No Pain

The women in the following stories are finding a new relationship with their bodies. Ironically, this journey takes them back on an ancient road, to a time when the rhythm of her cycle gave guidance and direction to a woman's total life. Imagine yourself several thousand years ago, a young girl who is the center of a celebration. You live in a prerecorded time when you are a guest of the Mother, the Goddess, the Earth. You see Her in everything about you and in yourself. You see Her in the seasons, the winds, the rocks, and the trees. You revere your body and your home as part of the rhythm, the cycle, the miracle. With each full moon, the women begin their monthly cycle of fertility, and you become a part of it. To welcome you to the circle, the women offer their flow to the Earth, in thanks, and now you are a woman.

Flash forward a few thousand years, to a culture where the Earth has been divided into private property. You live in a city where trees are the occasional ornament and the air is soiled. You seldom touch actual ground. You learn from a textbook that your body will change, but you are ill-prepared for the transition. No one speaks of your bleeding, except as a joke; you feel your womanhood as a burden.

Perhaps there is a relationship between shame, dark secrets, and pain.

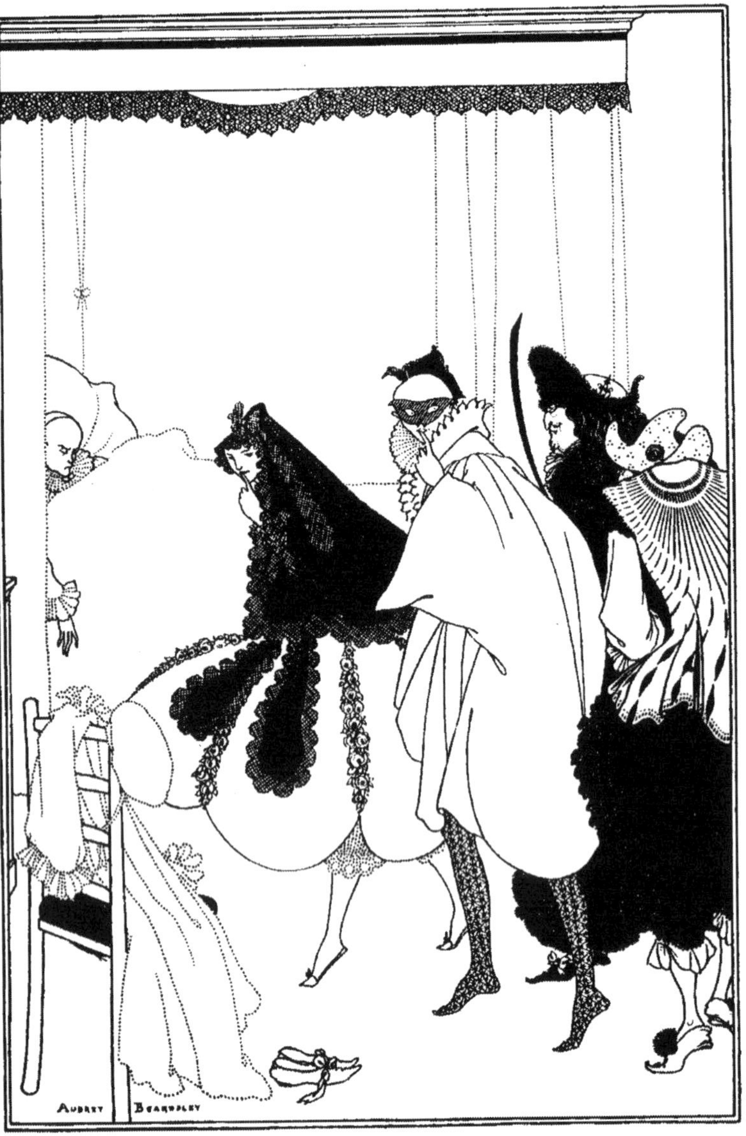
AUBREY BEARDSLEY

# A Little Magic

"I have never suffered the pain and humiliation associated with the female cycle that seem to plague other women, even though I was raised in California — the state of movie stars and swimsuits, where youth and glamour are a major industry. Amidst all this ersatz, I was raised pagan. My blood was seen as beautiful, a symbol of female sacredness and regenerative power. My menstruation has always been easy, painless, and welcome."

# Many Moons

"I have read that multiple personalities have been known to have several periods every month, one for each personality.

"Imagine being a woman with multiple personality disorder. Trying to manage a household and family is difficult enough with just one personality subject to periodic mood swings. But just think of coping while changing from personality to personality, each with her own set of memories, each with completely different health problems, and each with her own menstrual cycle. No wonder Sybil went for help. But what this clearly shows us is a body-mind connection that cannot be dismissed. Our mind, not just our brain, can exert a physical influence on our body and its cycles."

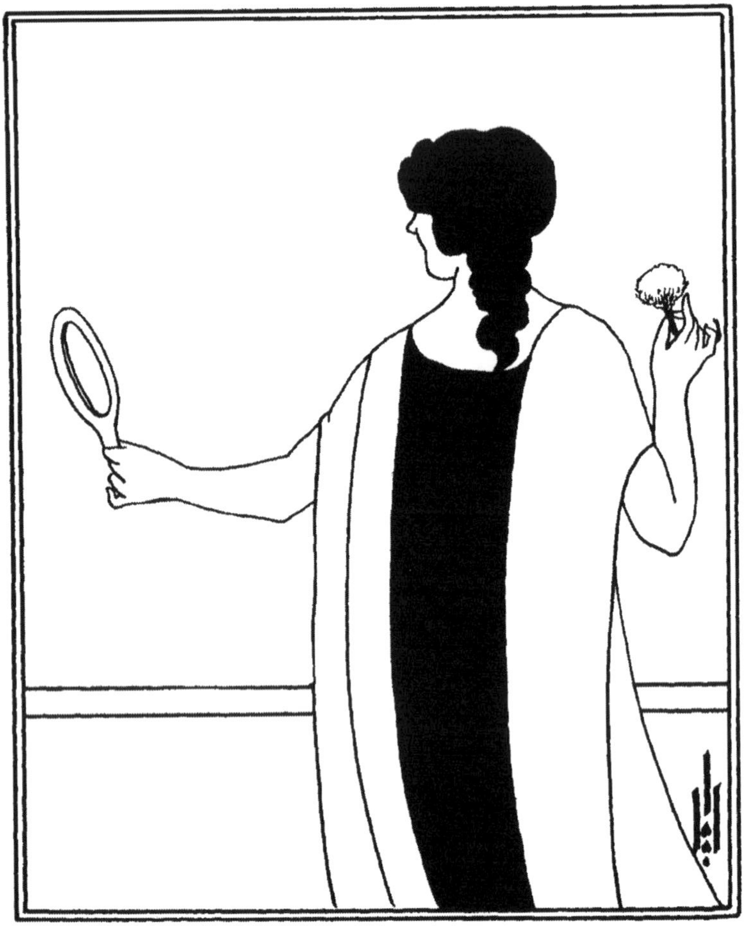

# All New and Improved

"The other day my daughter and her friends were watching MTV together in the family room. I was cooking dinner in the kitchen and could eavesdrop on them. As they tossed popcorn into their mouths, they came up with comments about the 'babes' in the music videos. The skimpy clothes on the pelvic-thrusting dancers, and the sexual lyrics of the songs, would lead you to believe that kids' culture today is one of totally uninhibited attitudes. Although I'm not wild about today's explicit and tasteless airing of sexual activities on television and in motion pictures, I wonder if this candor could be a healthier influence on kids than the uptight sexual secrecy in which I was raised — secrecy that caused me to feel shame about my body and its functions.

"My daughter and her friends listen attentively to ads for Maybelline and Clearasil, just like I used to do as a teen. But they also listen to public service announcements telling them to stay off drugs and practice safe sex. A commercial came on with a perfectly groomed young woman talking about the merits of Playtex tampons with odor control.

"I was raised on TV commercials from Playtex telling me that they could lift and separate my breasts with a Cross Your Heart bra, and how their girdle, with its 'fingertip panels,' would gently hold in the bulge of my round tummy. But a Playtex commercial advertising tampons in the middle of the *Dinah Shore Show*? Or *Loretta Young*? That would have been absolutely unthinkable."

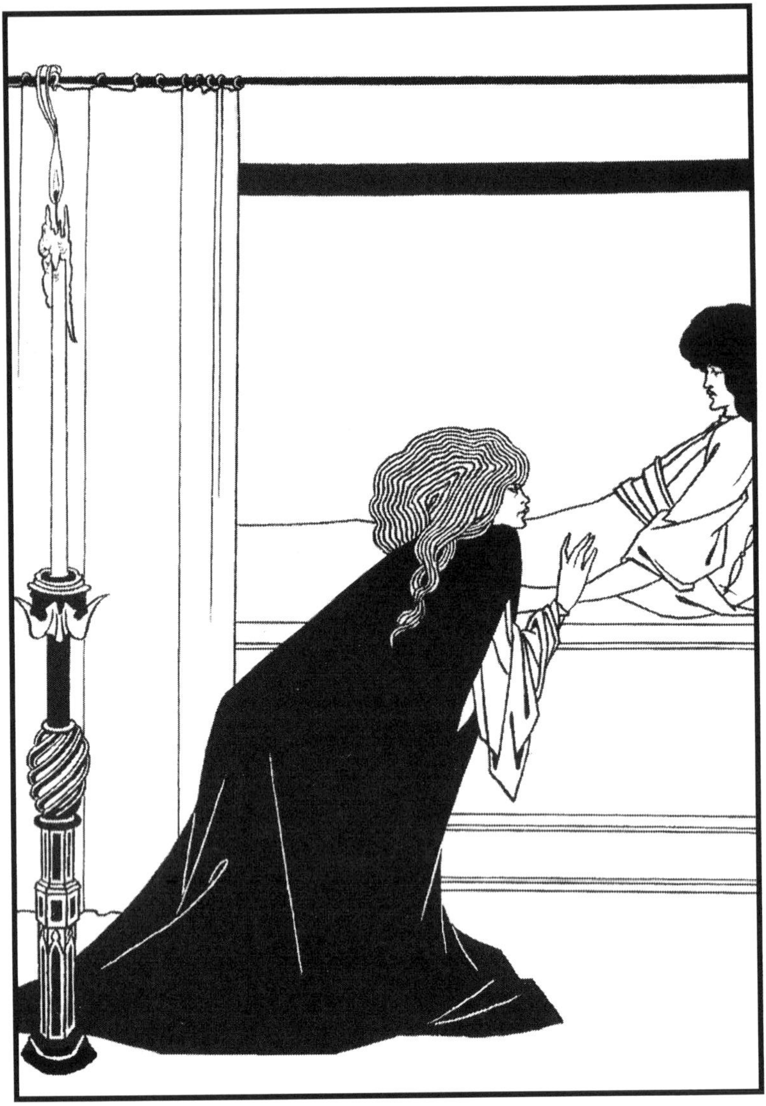

# Is It Terminal?

"I'll never forget the first time a friend told me she had PMS. I knew any disease that was referred to by its initials alone was a serious problem — TB, AIDS, MS, TMJ, or SIDS were nothing to sneeze at. I asked her what was wrong and how long she had been ill. When she told me it was a condition just before her monthly period that made her irritable and depressed, I just gave her a blank stare. I had heard of porphyria, which turns urine blue, and Tourette's syndrome, which causes uncontrollable talking, so I was not unfamiliar with exotic and rare diseases. When she said that 40 percent of all women suffer from PMS, it seemed odd that I had never heard of it.

"I thought about my own cycle and wondered whether I had been suffering all along and just hadn't realized it. But, even though on a typical day I can convince myself that I'm exhibiting at least five of the seven warning signs of cancer, I was sure I had never sensed a premenstrual syndrome. As the media began to cover PMS over the years, many friends came out of the closet. They now use PMS as a verb, as in 'Don't mind me, I'm just PMSing today,' and everyone understands the meaning. But I still wonder how a condition so pervasive could have gone unnamed for most of mankind's history."

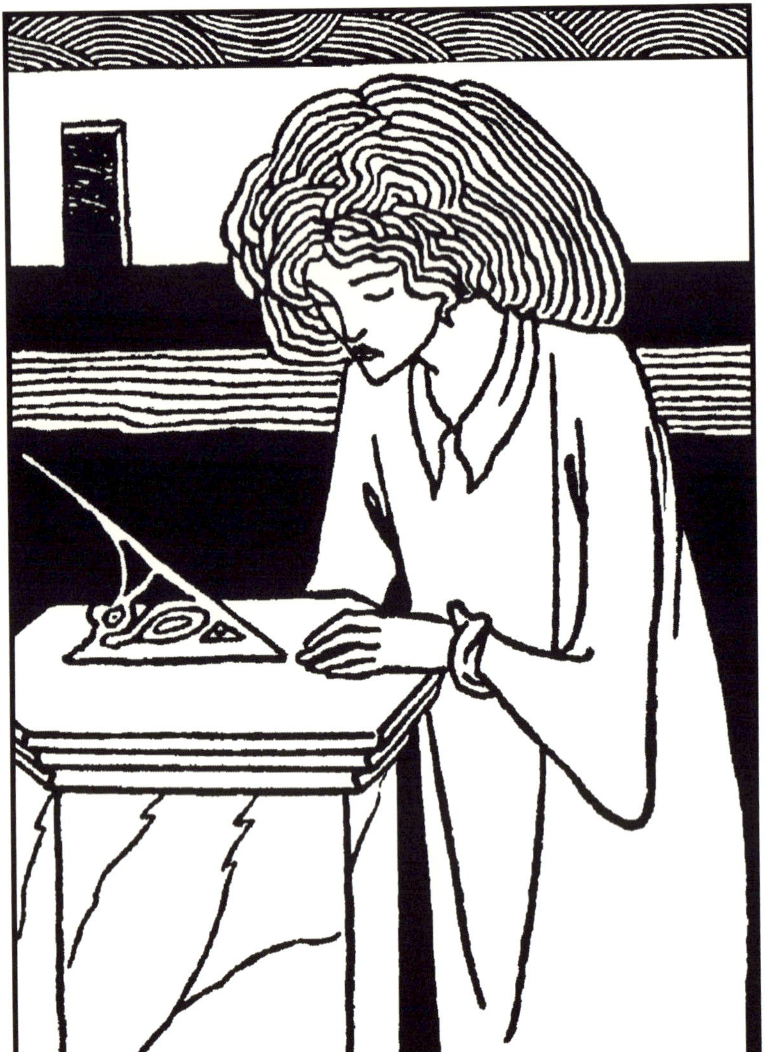

# Pins and Needles

"I always laughed at the *Saturday Night Live* skit in which Jane Curtin as Mrs. Lubner talked to Gilda Radner, playing her daughter, about 'that time of the month.' She used to say, 'It's a blessing, Lisa, and it's a curse.' I couldn't have agreed more. When Bill and I were first together, we didn't have the knowledge or the good judgment to use any protection. So I would sweat bullets every time I was late because I was scared to death that I was pregnant. On the day the flow would finally start, I saw it as the greatest blessing.

"After we had been married for six years and had our home and finances established, we decided to have a baby. I was surprised when I didn't get pregnant the first month I stopped using birth control. But no matter, we just knew we would be shopping for a crib and stroller before long. After the first year of trying, I did start to view my periods as a curse. Each month I would hold out hope that I was pregnant, only to be heartbroken on the twenty-eighth day. Infertility treatment wasn't really common yet, but we were fortunate enough to be able to adopt two children. These days, I don't see my periods as either a blessing or a curse. I don't pray for them to come or not come. I just trust that someone upstairs has the whole situation well under control."

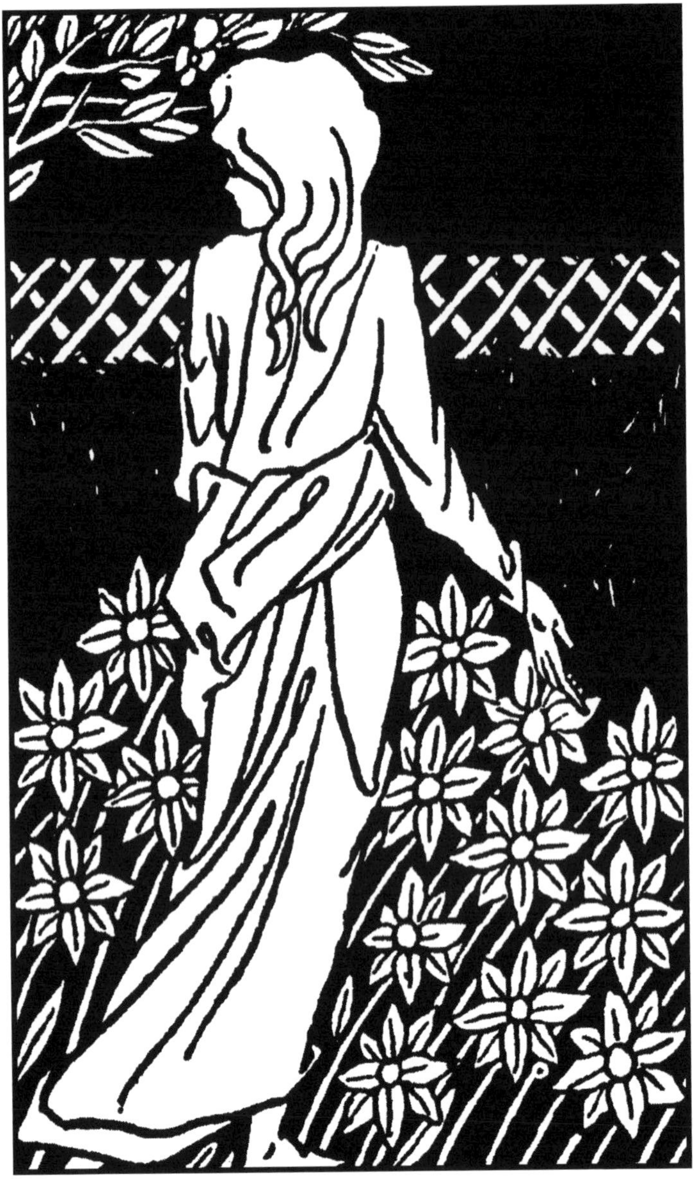

# Rags Revisited

"Although I'm not old enough to have been a flower child in the sixties, I went through what I think of as my 'Herbal Period' in the eighties. I grew out the hair under my arms, used a salt rock for deodorant, and tossed any cosmetics not designated cruelty-free. I sorted every scrap of garbage for recycling, even down to pulling the cellophane windows out of the envelopes before taking them to the recycling station. I took my own canvas grocery bag to the organic market where I bought granola sold to raise funds which would help save the rainforests. The only materials I couldn't figure out how to recycle were my tampons.

"Then one day, I went to my natural foods market to buy some organic tofu and noticed a product called 'Glad Rags,' 100-percent cotton reusable pads that came with colorful holders. What a cute name and what a wonderful idea. I invested in several and took them home. I am sorry to say that my ecological commitment lasted exactly one month. First of all, I had no idea where to put the used pads. I couldn't throw them in the laundry hamper with the other clothes and let them sit until I had a full load. So I had to wash them out whenever I changed pads, which meant when I was away from home, I had to deal with soggy pads. I used baggies to keep them from getting everything else wet in my purse. I decided very quickly that using all the soap and water to wash the pads and wasting plastic bags to carry them around was probably worse for the environment than just tossing a tampon."

*Feeling No Pain*

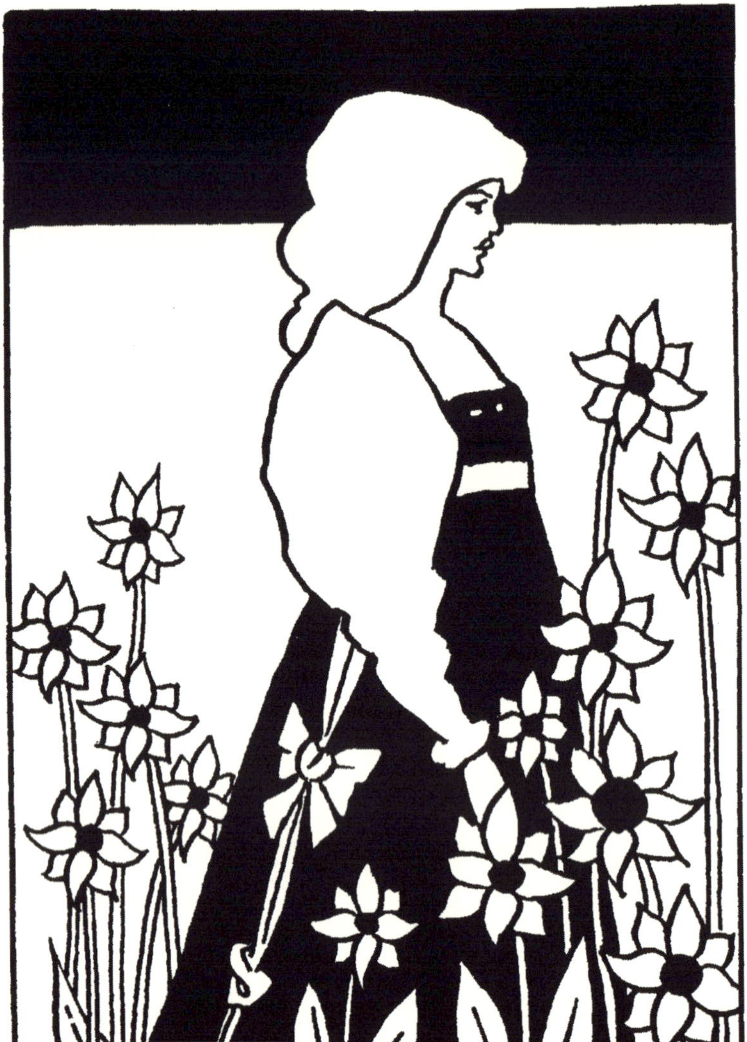

# My First Moon

"My mom sometimes gets carried away with her one-sixteenth Navajo blood. Like, she wanted to have a First Moon ceremony for me to 'welcome me into the sisterhood' when I started my periods. I told her no way. You have to understand, if she's told me once, she's told me a hundred times how her mother never explained the facts of life to her. She was only eleven when she started her periods, and she found out by surprise. But just because she's still mad at her mother about that doesn't mean she has to take it out on me. It's not that I'm embarrassed or anything dumb. My friends and I talk about that kind of stuff all the time. We even talk about it with guys, because they're cool with it. It's just that we don't want to discuss it with parents, because they get too weird about it.

"So when Mom wanted to send out invitations for this little Mummy-Daughter ritual, I asked her why she just didn't pin a note on my shirt that said I was now ovulating. She couldn't understand why I wasn't excited about women's magic and the wonder of bloody underpants. I don't know what folklore book she dug up this rite of passage idea from, but until I see it on TV, read about it in YM, or one of my friends does it first, I want no part of it. Meanwhile, Mom can connect with her ancestors by growing some corn or buying a loom. When I told her I'd compromise and let her honor my moon cycle if she let me get my nose pierced, she backed right off."

*Feeling No Pain*

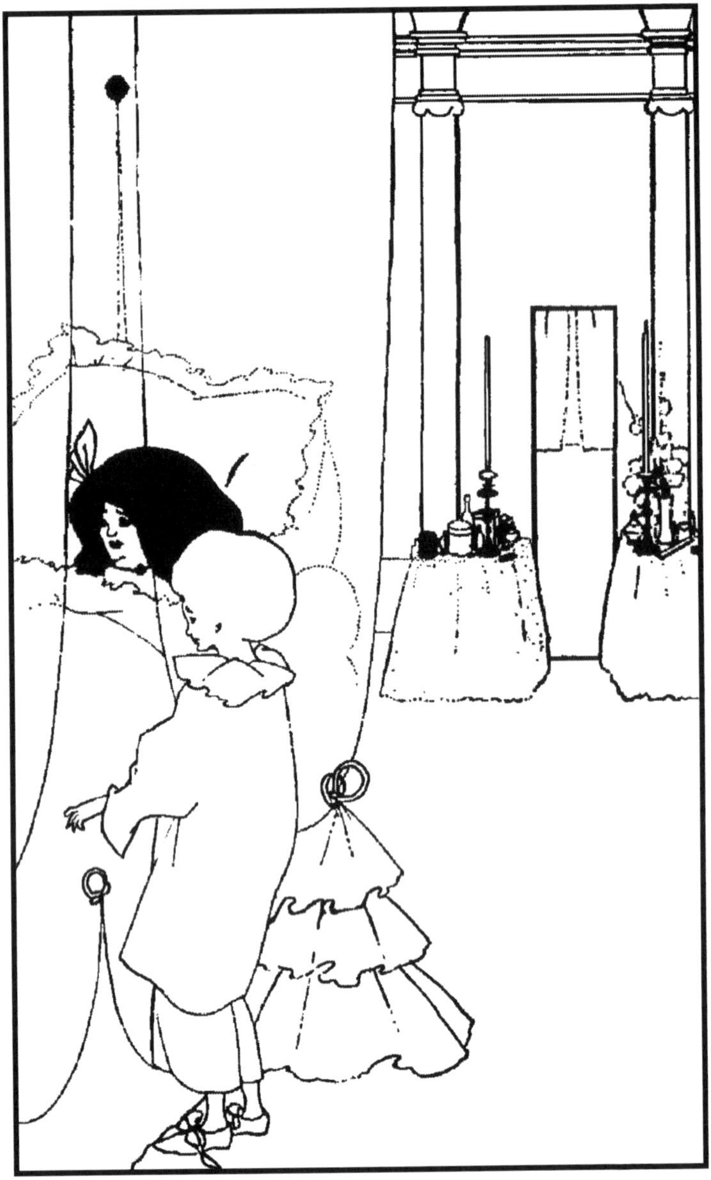

# Red Cross and Leeches

"I changed my thinking about my monthly cycle drastically when I read that our arteries become lined with cholesterol as a protective function from the toxicity of excess iron in the blood. I think the reason women are not as prone to heart disease until after menopause is because the monthly bleeding removes the excess iron from the body. Of course, this creates a danger of anemia, to which women are very susceptible. The medieval prevention for heart disease was for men to be bled at the change of seasons, to remove 'old' blood as the Earth was changing. Maybe there was some wisdom in this. The modern version is for men to donate blood once or twice a year.

"Taking blood out of the system removes a quantity of excess iron and forces the body to produce fresh new blood. It is also a way to gradually remove blood-borne environmental toxins from the body. This means our monthly periods are actually doing women a favor. It also means it would be a good idea to periodically donate blood after menopause. Heck, you're doing yourself a favor, as well as someone else."

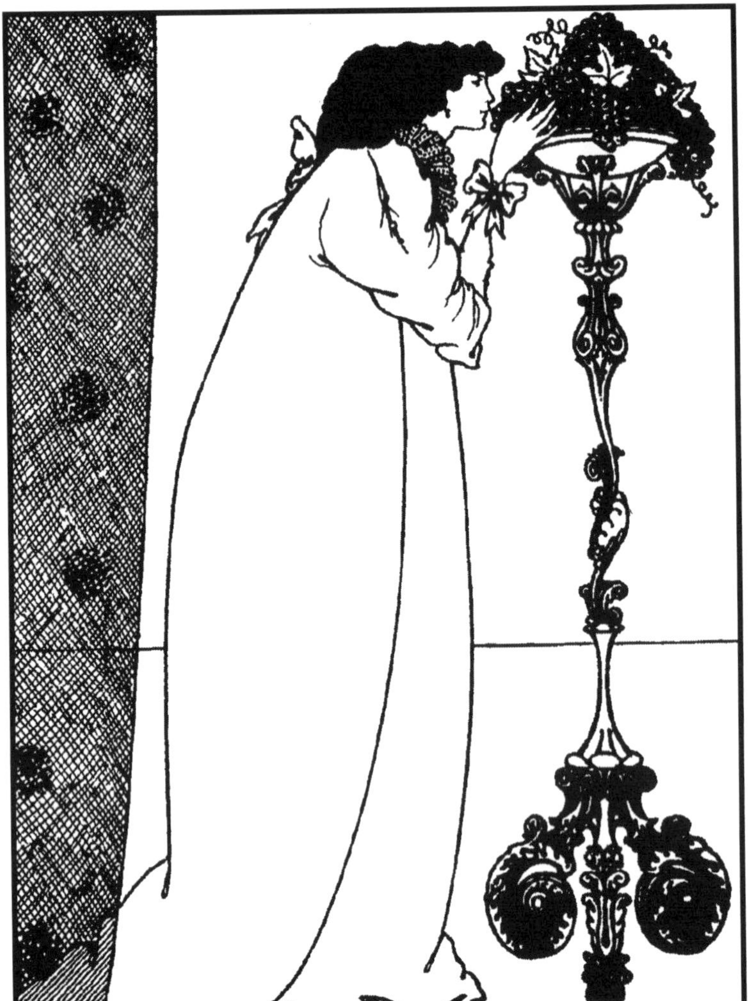

# PMS No More

"PMS is the manifestation of negative feelings about femininity. You punish yourself for being female. I used to have terrible symptoms, until I went on an internal, emotional campaign to rid myself of any sexual repression or negative self-image about being female. I decided that my moon-time was truly the time of my greatest magical power, as the wise women say. I realized that every month, I was using the irritable energy to go on a campaign to root annoyances out of my life. Before each period, I was standing up for myself and claiming my territory more fully. I was reclaiming my own sacredness and power and emotionally clearing myself so the magic of my bleeding could have a clear place to manifest.

"I stopped using tampons and began using small sea sponges instead. I got to know my own body, handled my blood and made peace with it. Now I have discovered how powerful it truly is. I treat it as a sacred fluid, returning it to the earth. My flow comes as a surprise, and the time between has gotten longer. I rarely have any symptoms, and even the cravings have decreased. I don't get yeast infections anymore either. Now I see my periods as my body gathering strength for the power time."

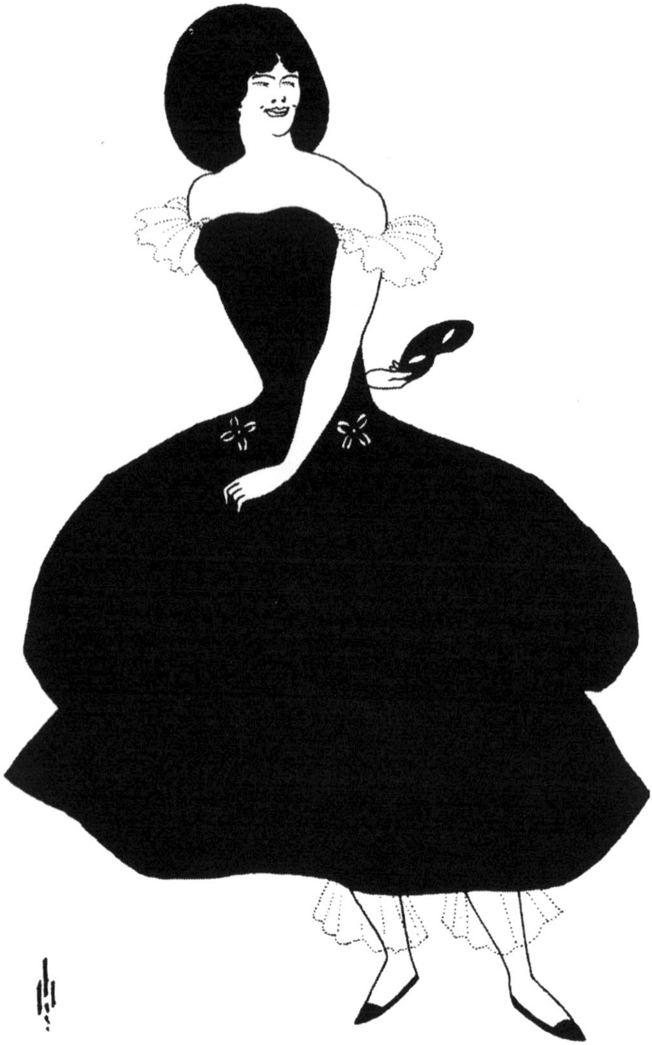

# Party On

"Matriarchal religions tend to be permissive, using the power of sexual energy for magical purposes, like making the crops grow better by sharing sexual energy on a full moon in the fields. They also tend to focus on worship of the body as a sacred vessel. Because Goddess is everywhere, including ourselves, we should follow the instincts She gave us and worship Her with love and pleasure.

"The patriarchal God, on the other hand, is up there in Heaven disapproving of us physical mud people having sex. For patriarchal religions to overpower the more ancient matriarchal religions, they had to suppress all trappings of the sacred power of sex. Women had to be programmed to believe even their sacred moon blood was unclean and sinful, a sign of weakness instead of a sign of their power and fertility. For patriarchal religions to dominate, it was essential that the best sources of true awakening be suppressed because awakened folks have direct evidence of the Goddess within and cannot be controlled or convinced otherwise. People who are spiritually awakened cannot listen to outside authority telling them things that disagree with their own spirit. Asceticism and deprivation are difficult paths to enlightenment. Your body knows that the quickest path to Goddess is through pleasure, even if She has to eroticize patriarchal sexual guilt and punishment to get Her messages through."

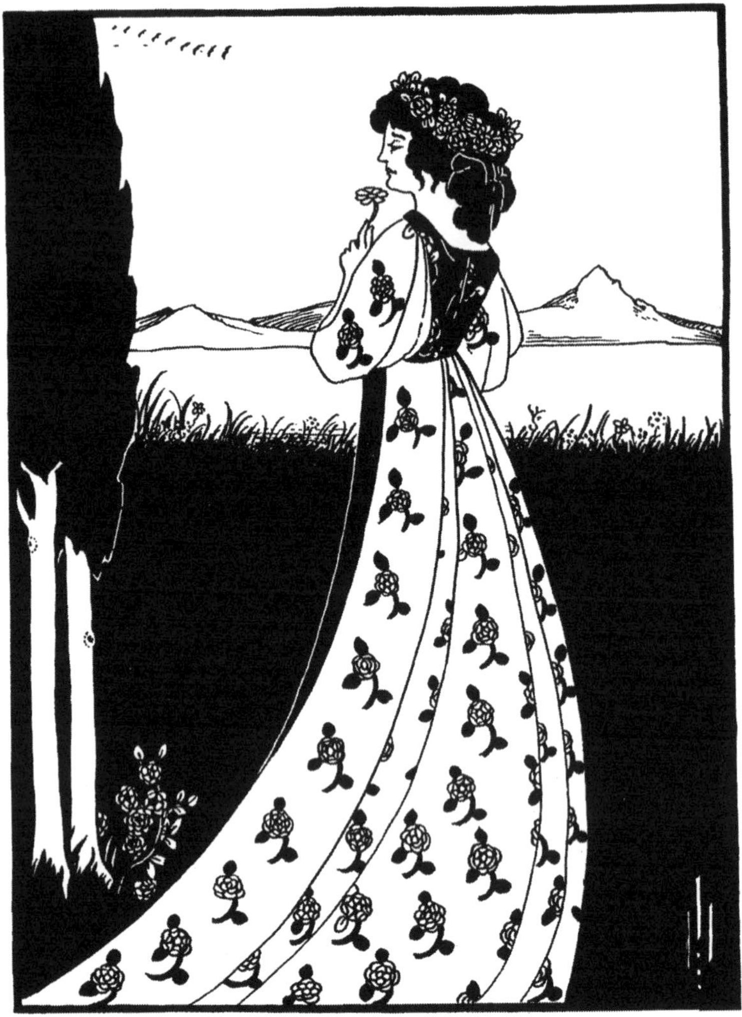

# Daughters of Eve

"In an effort to be equal to men, feminists often distance themselves from 'essential' female capabilities such as birthing, lactation, and menstruation. Many eco-feminists are proud of women's unique biology, and believe that equality with men should not come at the expense of sacrificing our special differences. In this regard, women of EVE (Eco-feminist Visions Emerging) organized a monthly gathering called Selene Circle to explore and celebrate the ancient primordial wisdom of women's ability to bleed.

"Selene Circle was named for one of the Greek goddesses of the moon, and women met on the new moon of each month. EVE women felt that we can directly contribute to deep planetary and personal healing by re-honoring the menstrual act. As many eco-feminists believe, all things in life — the moon, our blood, the oceans, pollution, starvation — are interconnected. Healing one part of our ecology helps heal other parts."

— Cathleen and Colleen McGuire, *EVE Online*

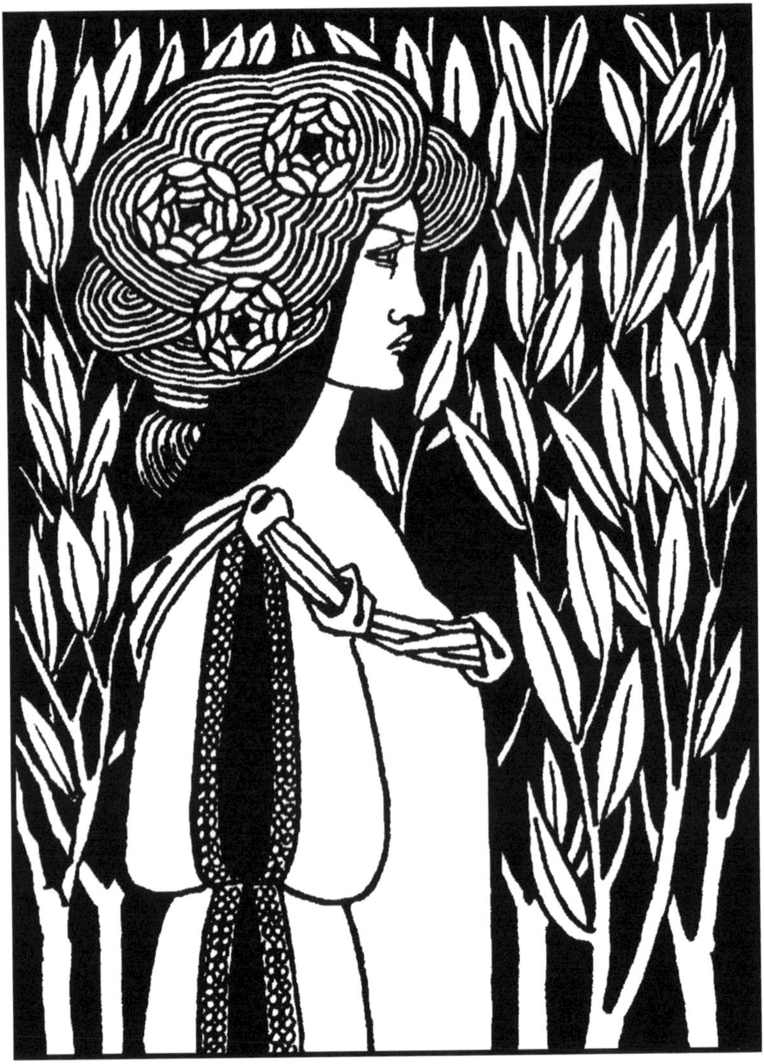

# Nature's Way

"As a natural healer, for PMS I recommend evening primrose oil or one of the lovely women's moon teas which you can usually find in health food stores. Dong quai will bring on the menstrual cycle, but it also has energizing effects and can cause sleeplessness. The hawthorn berry is for healing the heart and for menstrual discomfort. I also recommend red raspberry leaves for cramps. I tell my clients to avoid using bleached tampons, as they have been identified as a potential cause of ovarian cysts. I always recommend using unbleached tampons or reusable cotton pads rather than the commercial brands containing dioxin.

"Once woman's power, evidenced by her ability to bleed without being weakened, was revered. These were sacred mysteries. The only way to take away a woman's power is to persuade her to reject it herself. The Earth is my mother, the source of my strength, and my monthly cycle is part of her sacred rhythm.

"Rather than trying to numb my brain with a Midol, I try to make my moon time one of healing. As Chief Seattle said, 'All things are connected like the blood which unites one family. All things are connected. Whatever befalls the earth befalls the sons of the earth. Man did not weave the web of life: he is merely a strand in it. Whatever he does to the web, he does to himself.'"

# Cosmic Cramps

"One evening I was watching television, cuddled with a heating pad for my monthly cramps, and I listened to Peter Jennings as he reported on World News Tonight that NASA satellites had actually photographed the 'pulse and heartbeat of the planet Earth.' Through time-lapse photography, the changing temperature and moisture patterns of the entire planet were shown through the changing seasons. And sure enough, there it was on the evening news, the heartbeat of Earth.

"That night, I had an interesting dream about the planet as an organism with counterparts to the human body. Of course, the rainforests were the lungs, manufacturing oxygen for our global atmosphere. While a billion smokers burn their own lungs and suffer the consequences of lung cancer and emphysema, we also burn the planet's rainforest lungs and begin to feel its disease.

"I saw the Middle East, the cradle of civilization, as the womb of the Earth. In a time when the majority of women suffer menstrual pain and PMS, the Earth's own womb is now the center of great emotional and physical pain from continual warfare.

"I saw Africa, the Earth's stomach, suffering famine and starvation.

"America was the planet's heart, the core of its circulation. This nation, where the leading cause of death is heart disease, was symbolic of a planet sick at heart.

"The malignancies and systemic cancers that mankind suffers I saw tied to the radioactive poisoning of Earth by nuclear testing and inadequate disposal of radioactive waste.

"And the Earth's breasts, the symbol of the giving of life force, I saw nurturing humankind with acid rain and biologically dead rivers, while increasing numbers of women suffer breast disease.

"In my dream, the Earth struggled to balance her body by controlling the human pests. Infertility is increasing amongst the high income population while careless pregnancies of women living in poverty produce children who cannot be fed. And the Earth had an immune system which saw humans as destructive invaders. The AIDS virus was acting as planetary T-cells, working to curb man's destructiveness by destroying his own immune system.

"And where did the Earth purge? Into my dream came the image of the Dalai Lama, with his mission of compassion for all sentient beings.

"If dreams really are symbolic messages, then I know this dream was my message to start healing. The next time I have menstrual cramps, rather than feeling sorry for myself, I will use the opportunity to pray for healing in the Earth's womb—the Middle East."

*Feeling No Pain*

# A Rose Is a Rose

Menstruation must be an unusually unpleasant word because women have come up with just about every other term imaginable to avoid saying the 'M' word. Here is just a sampling of the code language women have developed to communicate without saying "menstruation":

| | |
|---|---|
| the curse | Granny |
| my time | dripping |
| the visitor | packing a sandwich |
| my monthly | my friend |
| Mabel | hemorrhaging |
| Aunt Mildred | the scourge |
| Uncle Charlie | leaking |
| on the rag | out of commission |
| indisposed | riding the crimson tide |
| flooding | on duty |
| Aunt Flo | my "favorite" time |

One woman spoke of the elaborate code she and her friends used:

*We always used to say that Mother Nature was coming to visit. If you were having bad cramps, you said that Mother Nature was packing heavy suitcases. If you were feeling okay, you said that Mother Nature had brought light luggage. When you were almost finished with your period, you said that Mother Nature was packing up to leave.*

A group of high school girls devised their own agreed upon code while riding on a ski bus one day:

*We decided the best metaphor for our uterus would be a dog. When we were having a period, we would say our dog was sick. If we had bad cramps, we would say our dog was throwing up. If we needed to borrow tampons, we would ask each other for dog bones.*

What if we had a more positive set of euphemisms for menstruation? Wouldn't we dread it less? How about these for starters:

| | |
|---|---|
| balancing | being feminine |
| celebrating | following Nature |
| going with the flow | cooperating with the Universe |
| cleansing | renewing |
| lucky days | restoring |
| releasing | Hot Mama |

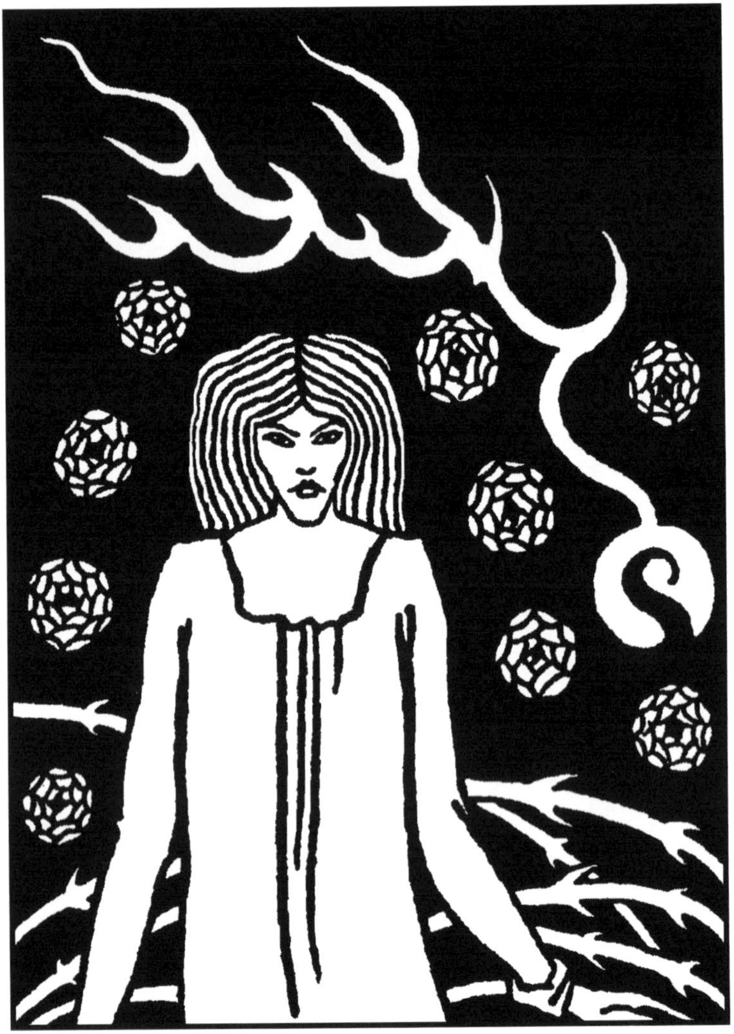

# Part Six
# The Power
# And the Punishment

In many diverse cultures, menstruation is strictly a taboo subject. In some, it is clouded in fantastic superstitions. Yet in other cultures, menstrual blood is seen as a powerful, even magic, substance. And in the rare matriarchal societies, it is revered and respected, as we imagine it was in the days of prehistory. Our only clue to those times has been the legacy of thousands of tiny statuettes of lactating and pregnant women. Perhaps these show us how the ordinary female cave dweller looked during most of her brief adult life, with menstruation being infrequent and mysterious.

In this section, we take a look at diverse cultural customs and attitudes, as well as menstrual synchrony and dysfunction on six continents.

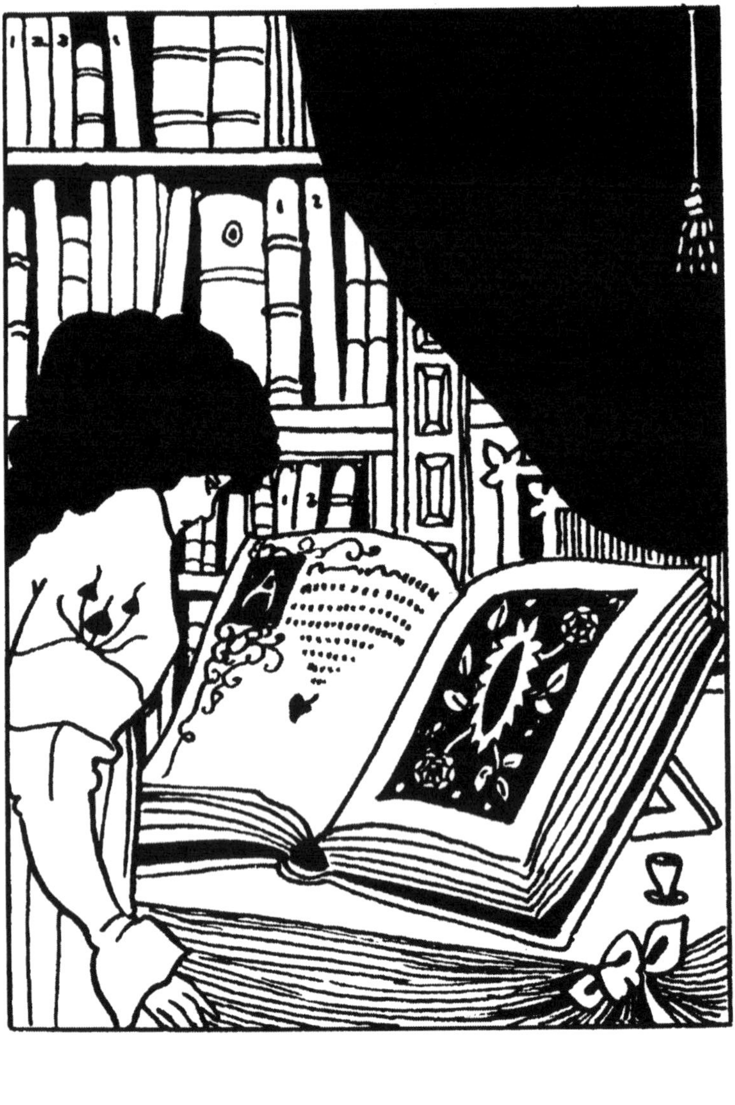

# Magical Menstrual Tour

Menstrual taboos are found all over the world, and sometimes even involve powerful sorcery or witchcraft. Many indigenous cultures prohibit men from copulating with menstruating wives or eating food prepared by them. In Ghana, violating a menstrual taboo, such as allowing menstrual blood to touch an altar, is punishable by immediate death. A fetish with menstrual blood on it is a powerful protective charm. In New Guinea, a woman believes she can kill a man by poisoning his food with menstrual blood. In Uganda, a woman protects her menstrual blood, believing it could be used to make her sterile if it fell into the wrong hands. While menstruating, she believes she must not even pass by a pottery kiln, because she would cause the pots to crack. She believes she can spoil the brewing of beer. She cannot touch food with her own hands, but must eat with two sticks.

In Australia, as in other indigenous cultures, aborigine women menstruate together and isolate themselves. Their ceremonies are kept hidden from the men. Envying this power, the aborigine men conduct their own bleeding ceremonies. An incision is made on the underside of the penis. While the women are away conducting their secret rituals each month, the men reopen the incisions and bleed together, covering each other and bleeding back into the ground. The bloodier the ceremony, the more powerful. And of course, it is taboo for women.

# Oriental Ovulation

Taboos are prevalent all through the East. There are Sufi temples in India where menstruating women and dogs are specifically prohibited. Guards stand at the entrance of the temples to check the pulses of women who are entering to ensure they are not menstruating. A Shinto woman is unclean during menstruation and after childbirth and cannot be touched by a Shinto priest. A Hindu woman does not pray in or go anywhere near the praying shrine in her home when she menstruates. If a Buddhist monk is touched by a menstruating woman, he must go and immediately bathe. In China, the old belief was that menstrual blood could contaminate the streets and make them unsafe. In modern Chinese factories, however, giving women two days off each month for menstrual leave is becoming a common practice.

A Muslim girl has a free spiritual ride and is considered pure until she begins menstruating, but after that, she starts accumulating sins. So on goes the veil, and for the rest of her life she must keep her body hidden. The Koran (2:222) says, "They question thee (O Muhammad) concerning menstruation. Say: It is an illness, so let women alone at such times and go not unto them till they are cleansed." During her menstrual cycle, a Muslim woman may not touch a Koran, enter a mosque, or observe the fast of Ramadan. She must eat secretly, and her eating and drinking are considered shameful.

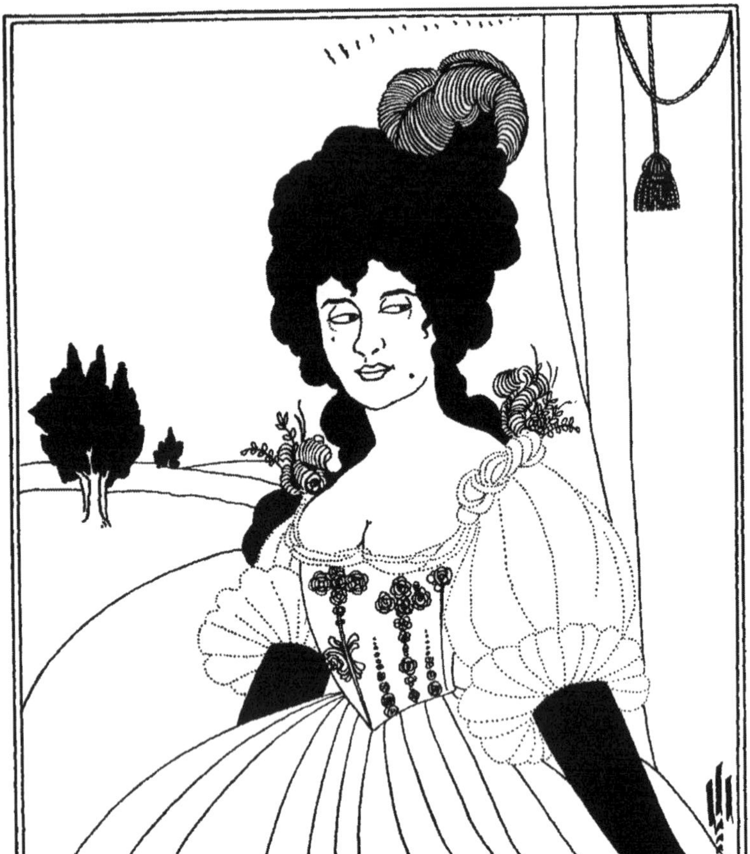

# The Western Womb

Western European peasant lore is full of taboos and superstitious beliefs that a menstruating woman can ruin crops, keep bread from rising, keep wine and beer from fermenting, spoil meat and dairy products, move objects, and contaminate religious ceremonies. Pliny wrote of the ancient Roman belief in the diverse powers of menstrual blood to ensure a good harvest and cure a wide variety of diseases — from goiters, gout, headaches and hydrophobia, to worms — and of men using menstrual blood to ensure the fidelity of their wives.

Some ancient superstitions have persisted. We find documents written in the early twentieth century alleging that a menstruating woman can be responsible for spoiling pickles, turning wine, withering plants, and causing bread to fall. There are records of physicians using menstrual blood in injections to treat the liver; and of using the menstrual blood of virgins in wound dressings. So, whether viewed as good or evil, menstrual blood is globally viewed as being a very powerful substance, physically and supernaturally.

# African Attitude

The Beng tribe of the Ivory Coast is a typical example of an indigenous tribe's menstrual customs. A menstruating Beng woman is not allowed to set foot in the forest, which is where the tribe works. She may not carry water or chop wood for the fires. A man may not eat any food cooked by a menstruating woman. No chores are allowed, except to stay in the village with the other menstruating women, cooking all day for themselves and enjoying each other's company. But the belief that menstrual blood carries in it a living being also brings powerful responsibilities to the Beng woman. If a married woman goes into the forest while menstruating, she will have a difficult delivery when she has her next child. If she defiles a field by entering it during menstruation, the crops in that field will die. If she is unmarried and has gone into the forest while on her period, when she marries, her father will sacrifice chickens and goats to the forest to apologize to the earth for the times she defiled it. If her father does not make the sacrifice before she becomes pregnant, she will have a difficult delivery. If the infant survives, it will be sickly or deformed. If a menstruating woman touches a corpse, she will have perpetual menstruation. She can even contaminate the logs of a fire if she touches any but her own. The belief in the power of menstrual blood affects every aspect of tribal life.

In another part of Africa, Sierra Leone, the ancient practice is to isolate a girl at puberty for a full year in a menstrual lodge, wherein she must take an oath upon her very life not to divulge the sacred women's mysteries she has learned. The custom is gradually dying out as an increasingly large number of African children attend school. The secret knowledge of the menstrual lodge, it turns out, is given to the children at school in their Health class.

# PMS, Pretty Mean Stuff

Anthropologists and sociologists debate about the causes of premenstrual syndrome. Although it has become a common experience for women in industrialized countries, it is not found in all cultures. Some researchers conjecture it is a result of increasingly high-fat diets combined with physical inactivity. Some feel it is because modern civilized woman simply has more periods in her life than a native woman whose periods are suppressed by sequential pregnancies and nursing infants, followed by an earlier death. Others argue that the monthly hormone changes responsible for ovulation and the subsequent sloughing of the uterine lining are also the cause for the mood and behavior changes.

Untreated PMS has even been offered as mitigation for murder in the legal system. Doctors can use hormone treatments which try to perfect the delicate balance of progesterone and estrogen, hormones so essential in driving out those monthly thoughts of homicide. But women can create chemical changes within themselves without the aid of medication. Mood is ultimately a chemical event partly determined by thoughts and emotions. Women tend to use very negative images and terms when they speak of their periods. Is it any wonder then that the impending onset of their menstrual cycle would bring on negative thoughts and emotions, which then manifest physically? Imagine if a man were sentenced to jail four days every month, with all the accompanying guilt, discomfort, and limitations. Wouldn't the monthly dread and frustration cause him to develop a pre-confinement syndrome similar to PMS? We would excuse him for a great many infractions on courtesy and compassion.

Many women who suffer from PMS describe the experience as "being possessed." In a culture that defines femininity as docile, compliant, patient, and caring, is it any wonder that the angry, assertive, and even sometimes violent person she becomes seems like an invading demon? Maybe it is nothing more than a negative attitude over the prospect of four days of pain, feeling unclean, and suffering in silence for fear of appearing the hypochondriac. Or maybe it could be, as some suggest, an autonomic rebellion against her feelings of being a second-class citizen.

*The Power and the Punishment*

# Menstruating Men

Writer Barbara Walker, in *The Crone*, writes of the position older women held in matriarchal societies as healer, teacher, and priestess.

"The collective unconscious of man holds a secret that woman seldom realizes. The secret may be too irrational for the practical female mind to grasp readily. However, those exquisitely detailed mirrors of the unconscious, mythology and religion, demonstrate the secret so thoroughly that it can hardly be doubted. The secret is this. In the hidden depths of men's minds, images of women are often identified with images of death…

"To the ancients it seemed obvious that the female principle is the only one that gives life. But every life so given mysteriously bears within it the seed of its own death. Thus, the life given and nurtured by the Great Mother, through the agency of the earthly mother, is necessarily finite. Mother gives a life that will be ended by death. Greedy man wanted more than this 'spangle of existence.' Growing too soon old and too late (if ever) enlightened, the one animal on earth able to realize its inevitable death often wasted its best years devising mental tricks to deny that realization.

"At every stage, man's images of woman were inextricably entangled with these ideas. First came the stage of birth giving and nurturing. Woman formed each new human life from her own interior 'wise blood'—that magical, taboo substance once believe to have descended from the moon, ever repeating the lunar phases. A mother voluntarily gave her whole attention to her helpless infant, day and night, for years, until the child could take a gradually increasing part in the life of the community. Ancient Hindu scriptures declared that a mother should be honored one thousand times more than a father because of her irreplaceable benevolence in bearing, nurturing, and training her child...

"After the male role in reproduction was finally recognized, castration of men for religious reasons was gradually abandoned—with a few well-known exceptions, such as the priests of Attis and the early Christian castrati; also, men Jesus mentioned as having made themselves eunuchs for the sake of the kingdom of heaven (Matt. 19:12). Still, ceremonial imitations of castration remained in general use, on the theory that father gods required these offerings. Circumcision was the usual substitute. It has been shown that the blood of circumcision was deliberately intended to correspond to women's life-giving 'moon-blood.' In Egypt, boys were dressed as girls for their circumcision ceremonies. In some primitive cultures even in the present century, it has been found that male genital mutilation (such as subincision) was referred to as 'man's menstruation,' the wound described as a vagina, and the whole purpose of the ceremony was said to unite each man with the spirit of the Mother. Australian aborigines painted themselves and their sacred paraphernalia red for religious rites, declaring that the red color symbolized menstrual blood. In southeastern Asia, the gods themselves derived their heavenly immortality from their intimate contact with the Great Mother's life-giving menstrual fluid."

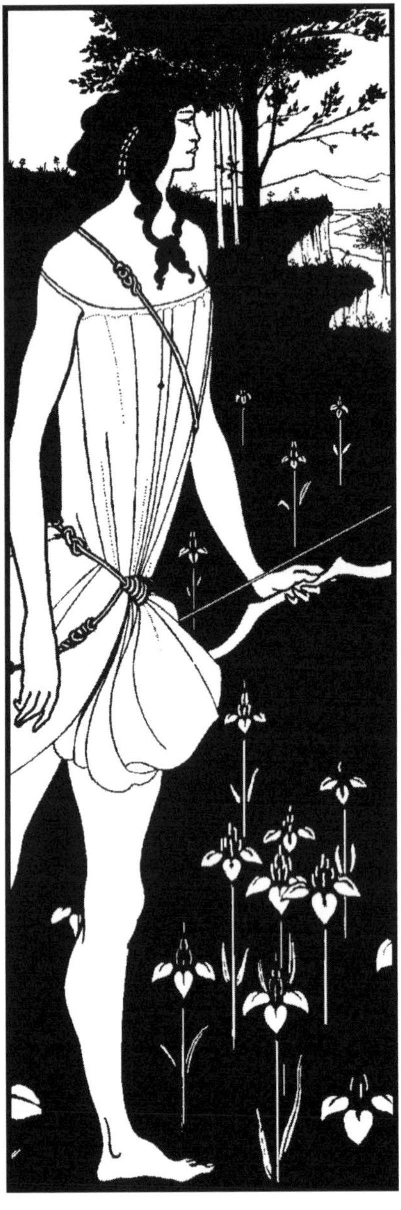

# Moon Lodge Mysteries

Native North American culture revolved around cycles: the daily cycle of the earth, the yearly cycle of the sun, and the monthly cycle of the moon. Each cycle was steeped in ritual and tradition, but the moon cycle was centered around women. The women of diverse Native American tribes practiced isolation during their moon cycle, a time when a woman was at the height of her creative power. There are some remnants of this tradition still practiced today. The woman's normally rigorous chores were limited to gathering firewood and performing ceremonial bathing rituals.

The moon lodge was a place of meditation, prayer, and spiritual growth. The fertile women of the tribe all menstruated together, and if a woman got out of this synchrony, she would sit in the moonlight and ask to be balanced back into the cycle. The women would commune with the spirits, and the female spirits were even said to be menstruating with the earth cycle. During this time, the men would go to the sweat lodge to train and build their own spiritual power, perhaps trying to compete with the women whose bodies naturally brought them monthly magic. The shamans of one Native American culture, the Lakota, request that women 'on their moon' not touch the sacred eagle feathers because during that time women are too powerful.

As a monthly moon ritual, a Quechuan shaman prescribes that the first day be spent in quiet meditation. On the second day, the Quechua women conduct a drum ceremony and place their hands and feet flat upon the ground to become a bridge between heaven and earth. They set out bathing water to absorb solar and lunar energy. At sunrise the next day, they perform ritual bathing — first the right leg, then the left leg, then the right arm, then the left arm, all the while visualizing being showered in pure light. On the fourth day, they sing, dance, and celebrate.

So, let's see how we could adapt this to our industrialized culture. Spend the first day of your period each month in isolation. Hmmm. You just call your supervisor to report you're taking a day of meditation for your moon cycle. Gee. Most supervisors would understand, unless of course your supervisor is a woman who is also home meditating on her own moon cycle. And the kids and husband should be no problem. Just put the Barnie video on auto-loop for the tots, and give Herb the stack of take-out menus. Then have yourself a tranquil meditation, knowing family and household will run smoothly without you.

On day two, bleeding on a tree should be no problem if you've got a fenced yard and go out before daybreak. You apartment dwelling ladies may have to commandeer a corner of a local park to offer your menstrual blood to a needy tree. You may need a permit of sorts, lest a local gendarme interpret a little too liberally the statutes against performing bodily elimination functions in public. You ladies could arrange group squats just like the good old pagan days.

Day three should be a piece of cake, assuming you remember to set out your bathing water the day before. Of course, in addition to solar and lunar energy, your water may also collect a fair amount of acid rain and pigeon droppings, assuming your dog or toddler doesn't get to it first.

Day four is the easiest of all. If your husband asks

why you're singing and dancing around the living room and you tell him you're celebrating your moon cycle, try to finish up before the ambulance arrives to escort you to your mental competency examination.

Unless maybe you're a hermit living somewhere in Wyoming, a monthly Quechuan Moon Ceremony might not fit smoothly into your routine. But maybe there's a compromise. What if you wrapped your box of tampons with pretty paper and a ribbon, so when you opened it, you acknowledged the gift your body gives you each month? What if you put a flower bud on your desk or nightstand on your moon days, just to remember you are part of a wonderful cycle? What if you just placed your gentle hands on your aching tummy, the way you would comfort a feverish child? What if you just dedicated those days to kindness and gratitude? You don't need a drum to celebrate. But if you'd like, drum on.

# The Red Tent

In her historical novel *The Red Tent*, Anita Diamant gives a fictional account of the Biblical character Rachel, who cannot be promised to Jacob until after the onset of puberty. She writes of an anxious Rachel, who impatiently awaits her entrance into womanhood. Diamant gives us a glimpse into the most ancient of women's rituals:

"She began to nurse dark fears about the future. She would never bleed, never marry Jacob, never bear sons. Suddenly, the small, high breasts of which she had been so proud seemed puny to her. Perhaps she was a freak, a hermaphrodite like the gross idol in her father's tent, the one with a tree stalk between its legs and teats like a cow.

"So Rachel tried to rush her season. Before the next new moon, she baked cakes of offering to the Queen of Heaven, something she had never done before, and slept a whole night with her belly pressed up against the base of the asherah. But the moon waned and grew round again, while Rachel's thighs remained dry. She walked into the village by herself to ask the midwife, Inna, for help and was given an infusion of ugly nettles that grew in a nearby wadi. But again the new moon came and again Rachel remained a child.

"As the following moon waned, Rachel crushed bitter berries and called her older sisters to see the stain on her blanket. But the juice was purple, and Leah and Zilpah laughed at the seeds on her thighs.

"The next month, Rachel hid in her tent, and did not even slip away once to find Jacob.

"Finally, in the ninth month after Jacob's arrival, Rachel bled her first blood, and cried with relief. Adah, Leah, and Zilpah sang the piercing, throaty song that announces births, deaths, and women's ripening. As the sun set on the new moon when all the women commenced bleeding, they rubbed henna on Rachel's fingernails and on the soles of her feet. Her eyelids were painted yellow, and they slid every bangle, gem, and jewel that could be found onto her fingers, toes, ankles, and wrists. They covered her head with the finest embroidery and led her into the red tent. They sang songs for the goddesses; for Innana and the Lady Asherah of the Sea. They spoke of Elath, the mother of the seventy gods, including Anath in that number, Anath the nursemaid, defender of mothers.

"They sang:
> *Whose fairness is like Anath's fairness*
> *Whose beauty is like Astarte's beauty?*
> *Astarte is now in your womb,*
> *You bear the power of Elath.*

"The women sang all the welcoming songs to her while Rachel ate date honey and fine wheat-flour cake, made in the three-cornered shape of woman's sex. She drank as much sweet wine as she could hold. Adah rubbed Rachel's arms and legs, back and abdomen with aromatic oils until she was nearly asleep. By the time they carried her out into the field where she married the earth, Rachel was stupid with pleasure and wine. She did not remember how her legs came to be caked with earth and crusted with blood and she smiled in her sleep.

"She was full of joy and anticipation, lazing in the tent for the three days, collecting the precious fluid in a bronze bowl — for the first-moon blood of a virgin was a powerful libation for the garden. During those hours, she was more relaxed and generous than anyone could remember her.

"As soon as the women rose from their monthly rites, Rachel demanded that the wedding date be set."

# Maidens and Mothers

At the beginning of the twentieth century, women began looking to self-improvement manuals for guidance. *Perfect Womanhood for Maidens — Wives — Mothers*, by Mary R. Melendy, M.D., Ph.D., is a "how to" book written in 1903, with advice for becoming the "perfect" woman, and remedies for menstrual complaints:

"The first appearance of the menses is generally preceded by the following symptoms: Headache, heaviness, languor, pains in the back, loins, and down the thighs, and an indisposition to exertion. There is a peculiarly dark tint of the countenance, particularly under the eyes, and occasionally uneasiness and a sense of constriction in the throat. The perspiration has often a faint or sickly odor, and the smell of the breath is peculiar. The breasts are enlarged and tender. The appetite is capricious, and digestion is impaired....

"Very much depends upon the regular and healthy action of the discharge, for to it woman owes much of her beauty and perfection. Great care should therefore be used to guard against any influences that may tend to derange the menses. Sudden suppression is always dangerous. Cold baths, foot baths, wetting the feet by the wearing of thin shoes, are very injurious during this period. A young woman anxious to attend a party or ball during this period sometimes takes a hip bath to arrest the discharge, but what a train of horrors follows such an insane act, and still there are many foolish enough to do this....

"An inordinate flow occurs generally in women of sanguine temperament, whose pulse is strong, and whose

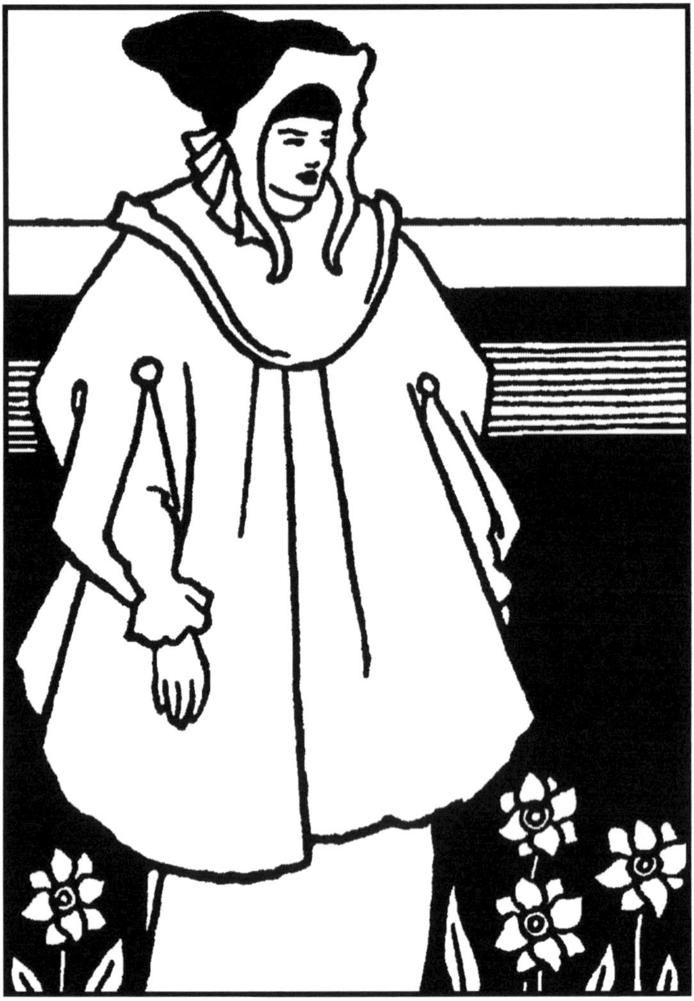

circulation is free; again where the passions are strong and exposed to over-excitation, reflex action might determine blood to the generative organs and induce congestion that nature relieves by profuse menstruation. The disease is also common among women of nervous, irritable temper; in those who are corpulent and of indolent habits; and those who live in hot climates or occupy rooms having a high temperature. Flooding from any cause, should be treated promptly, as serious consequences may follow its continuance. If flooding is severe, use hot water vaginal injections — hot as can be borne — once or twice a day. Take on alternate days the following remedies: Tincture of Iron — 3 drops in one full glass of water, two teaspoonfuls every hour. On the second day, take of tincture of Viburnum Opulus — 6 drops, Tincture of Belladonna — 2 drops, Peruvian Bark — 6 drops. Mix in full glass of water, two teaspoonfuls every hour....

"The suffering connected with [painful menstruation] is of the most intense and acute character, yet thousands of women periodically bear this torture, smiling during the short interval of ease that comes between the spasms. There is a pain-enduring capacity in woman that certainly man knows not of; in the throes of labor she smiles in anticipation of gladness. It is that struggle between the moral and physical from which woman comes out a heroine.

"Causes of Painful Menstruation — Taking cold during the period; fright, violent mental emotions; obstinate constipation; sedentary occupations; smallness of the mouth and neck of the womb. Women subject to this trouble are generally relieved by marriage."

# Fruit of the Womb

As Western culture developed, its myths were permeated with allusions to women's mysteries. Jennifer Barker Woolger and husband Roger J. Woolger explain, in *The*

*Goddess Within: A Guide to the Eternal Myths That Shape Women's Lives*, the menstrual symbolism of the myth of Persephone, who was abducted by Hades:

"When Perse-phone is in the underworld, she makes a bargain with Hades so that she can return to be with her mother, Demeter, for part of the year. She must remain with Hades for a number of months based on the number of pomegranate seeds she swallows, traditionally four, which is one third of the year. Given the blood-and-seed imagery of the fruit, it seems likely that this transaction also symbolizes the menstrual cycle, that part of the month when a woman's body must suffer the death of a potential life within her. Which is another way of saying that during the death phase of her cycle every woman must live with her inner Hades. When it is not made conscious in a woman's life, this inner encounter with the necessity of death can produce all kinds of menstrual and premenstrual difficulties. To honor Persephone is to honor the perpetual cycle of life and death...

"One of Demeter's teachings is that each woman, whether she bears children or not, must honor the monthly death and renewal that takes place in her body. It is an integral part of her cyclical nature as woman, as earth being bound mysteriously to the moon. Each month an ovum is released inside her and, except on a very small number of occasions in her life if at all, it will be shed, given back to the earth....

"Here is the meaning of the pomegranate of [Persephone]; when she goes underground, she discovers the rich red fruit with its clusters of bloodlike grapes, a perfect image of ovulation. It is a blood sacrament with the earth, no more, no less."

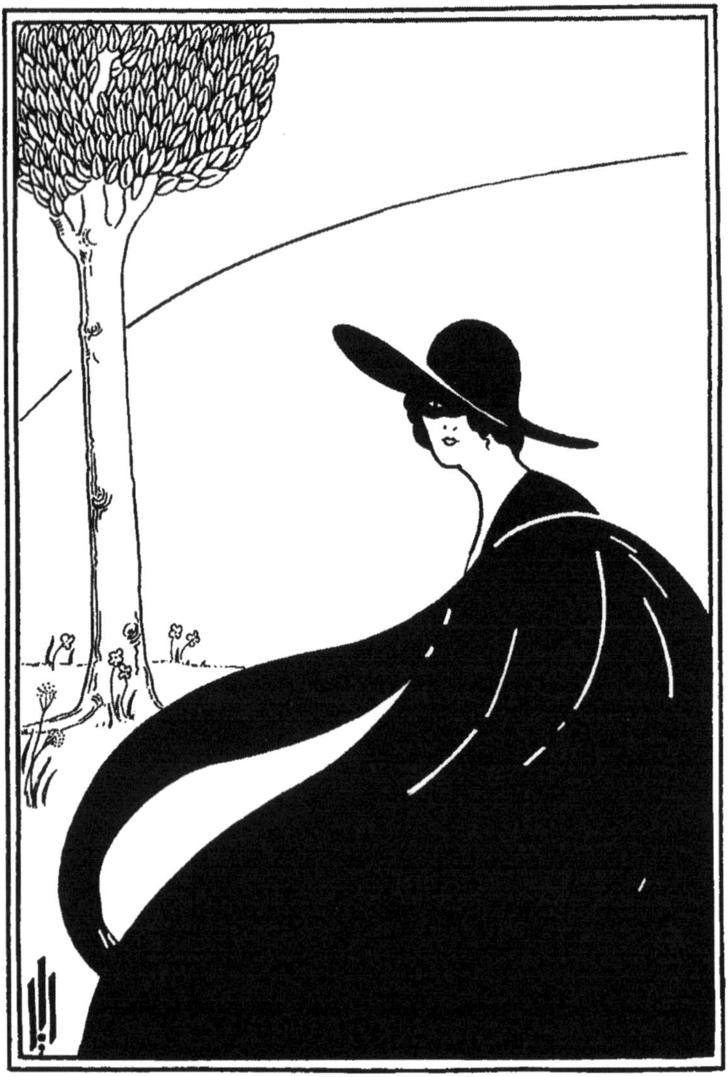

# The Great Secret

In her 1977 novel, *The Women's Room,* Marilyn French writes of puberty through the dark and defeated voice of a young girl who has had the secrecy of menstruation impressed upon her, a girl who does not see it — indeed, cannot see it — as a joyful event:

"At the end of her fourteenth year, Mira began to menstruate and was finally let in on the secret of sanitary napkins. Soon afterward, she began to experience strange fluidities in her body, and her mind, she was convinced, had begun to rot....

"...Suddenly her body had been invaded by a disgusting, smelly substance that brought pain to her lower half and anxiety to her mind. Could other people smell her? Her mother said she would have this the rest of her life, until she got old. The rest of her life! The blood caked on the napkin had chafed her. It smelled. She had to wrap it up in toilet paper — she used nearly a quarter of a roll — then carry it to her room and put it in a paper bag and later carry it downstairs and put it in the garbage. Five or six times a day for five or six days every month she had to do this. Her clean white smooth body had this inside it?... So men remained in charge of their bodies; they were not invaded by painful and disgusting and bloody events they could not control. That was the great secret, that was what boys knew and laughed at, that's why they were always poking each other and looking at girls and laughing. That was why they were the conquerors...."

# The End of Innocence

Two prominent female voices of the mid and latter twentieth century, Simone de Beauvoir and Camille Paglia, portray equally depressing views of the impact of menstruation on a woman's psyche in modern culture. In *The Second Sex*, French writer Simone de Beauvoir paints a grim portrait:

"At sixteen, a woman has already been through painful ordeals: puberty, monthlies, awakening of sexuality, first desires, first fevers, fears, disgusts, equivocal experiences; she has stored all this up in her heart, and she has learned to guard her secrets carefully.... It is not easy to play the idol, the fairy, the faraway princess, when one feels a bloody cloth between one's legs; and, more generally, when one is conscious of the primitive misery of being a body....

"...And though the first surprise is over, the monthly annoyance is not similarly effaced; at each recurrence the girl feels again the same disgust at this flat and stagnant odor emanating from her — an odor of the swamp, of wilted violets — disgust at this blood, less red, more dubious, than that which flowed from her childish abrasions. Day and night she must think of making her changes, must keep watch of her underwear, her sheets, must solve a thousand little practical and repugnant problems."

American writer Camille Paglia gives an equally grim and disenchanted viewpoint in *Sexual Personae: Art and Decadence from Nefertiti to Emily Dickinson*:

"Every month for women is a new defeat of the will. Menstruation was once called 'the curse,' a reference to the expulsion from the Garden, when woman was condemned to labor pains because of Eve's sin. Most early cultures hemmed in menstruating women by ritual taboos. Orthodox Jewish women still purify themselves from menstrual uncleanness in the mikveh, a ritual bath. Women have borne the symbolic burden of man's imperfections, his grounding in nature.... Or is it possible there is something uncanny about menstrual blood, justifying its attachment to taboo? I will argue that it is not menstrual blood per se which disturbs the imagination — unstanchable as that red flood may be — but rather the albumen in the blood, the uterine shreds, placental jellyfish of the female sea... Every month, it is woman's fate to face the abyss of time and being, the abyss which is herself."

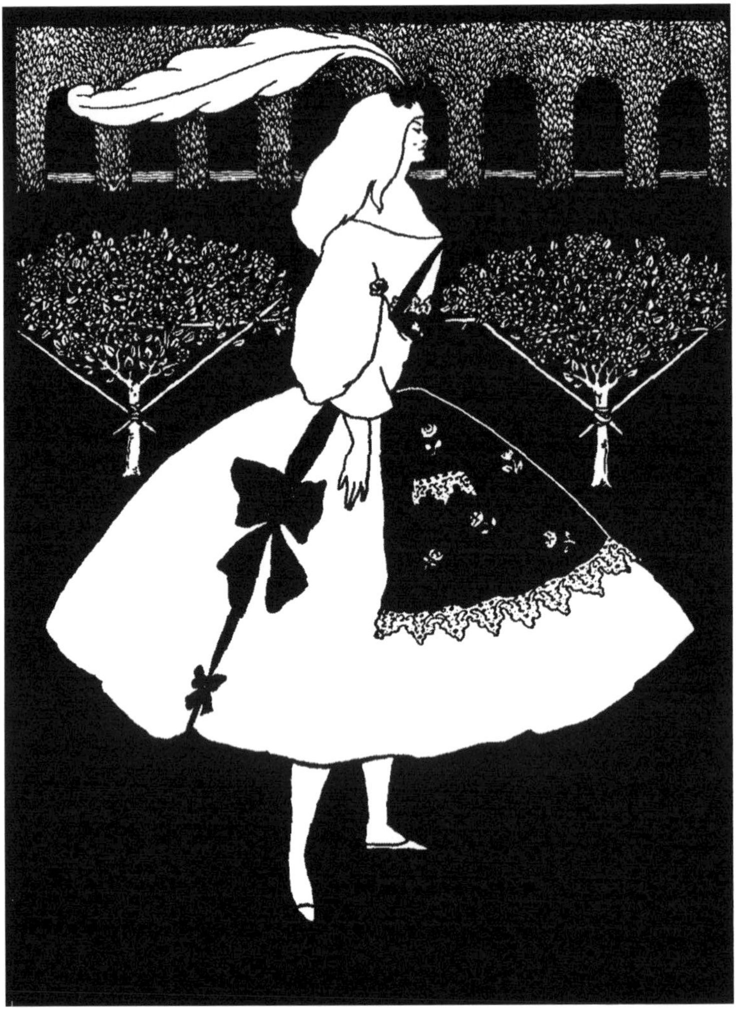

# An Act of Congress

"What would happen if suddenly, magically, men could menstruate and woman could not? Clearly, menstruation would become an enviable, boast-worthy, masculine event: Men would brag about how long and how much. Young boys would talk about it as the envied beginning of manhood. Gifts, religious ceremonies, family dinners, and stag parties would mark the day. To prevent monthly work loss among the powerful, Congress would fund a National Institute of Dismenorrhea."

Gloria Steinem

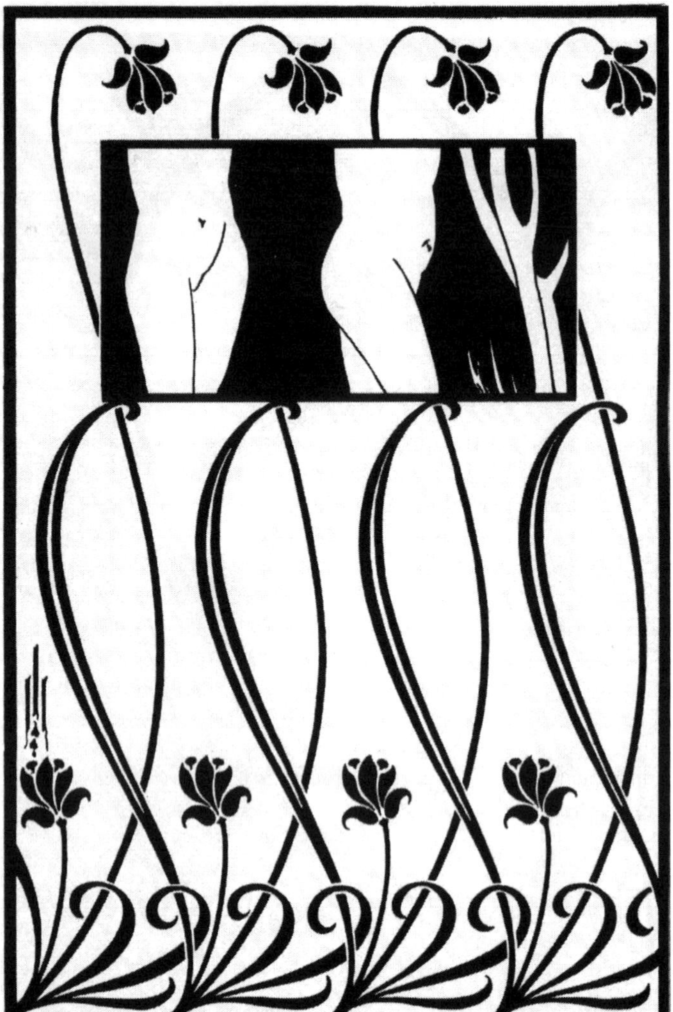

# Part Seven
# Ebb and Flow

Now, leaving the menstrual images we have read of swamps and slime, we turn to writers who include sociologists, clergy, and the diverse medical field, who speak of new approaches to healing the body and mind.

We will be shown more fully the connection between our relationship with the Earth and our own body's health.

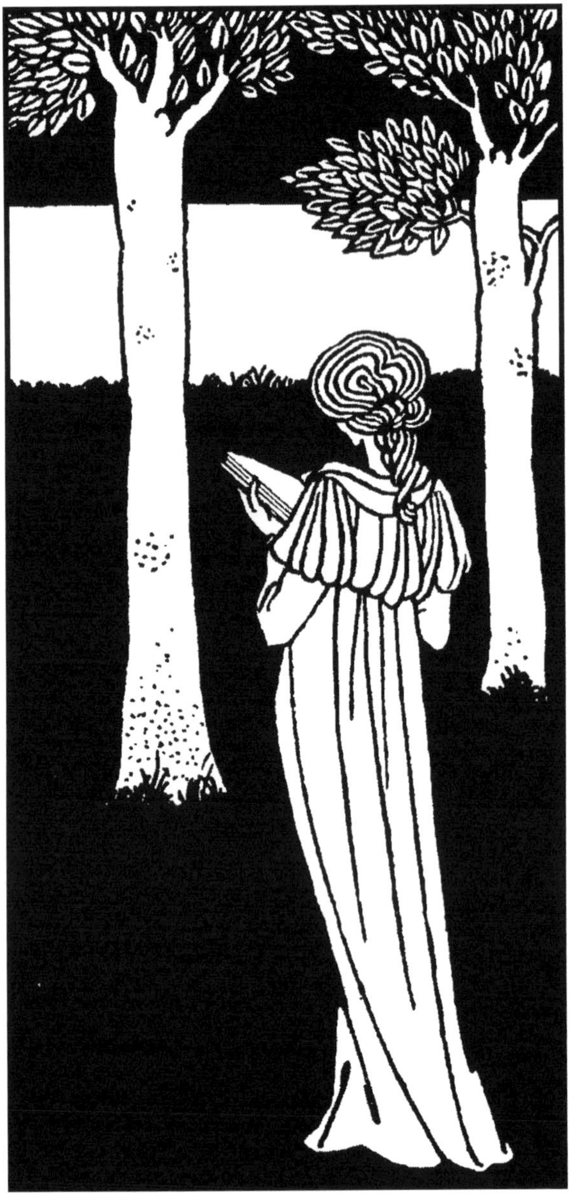

# A Young Voice Still Speaks

Diaries are sometimes the only source of consolation for the girl or woman who cannot bring herself to speak of her body to another. How many young girls have taken comfort from this single diary page of a young voice confessing her heart's secrets, and how many more will continue to read it throughout the years:

"I think what is happening to me is so wonderful, and not only what can be seen on my body, but all that is taking place inside. I never discuss myself or any of these things with anybody, that is why I have to talk to myself about them.

"Each time I have a period — and that has only been three times — I have the feeling that in spite of all the pain, unpleasantness, and nastiness, I have a sweet secret, and that is why, although it is nothing but a nuisance to me in a way, I always long for the time that I shall feel that secret within me again."

—Anne Frank, *The Diary of a Young Girl*

# Wise Wound

Penelope Shuttle and Peter Redgrove, in *Wise Wound: Eve's Curse and Everywoman*, write of the British term PMT, premenstrual tension, which is the same syndrome as the American PMS:

"Premenstrual tension may show all the opposites, good-bad, light-dark, love-hate. Impossibilities and alternatives may revolve with enormous energy and rapidity, then the period comes with its terrific discharge of tension and the whole matter is different. If this is done with conscious purpose, and not in the body alone, then the monthly struggle is not mere repetition of a forced situation. Experienced growth, creative turmoil and resolution, the anguish of choices, and the solution that comes of itself are all possible. 'Do nothing' is sometimes the best advice, but above all, not to fear....

"Women sometimes wish that men could feel what pre-menstrual tension is like. It is a feeling like nothing else, they say. It is a scratchy, jumpy state, your energy is gone, all the life drains out of the world, which becomes a 'sour apple,' you have no friends, your nerves seem to stick out six feet from your body, you feel bloated and heavy, but at the same time exquisitely nervous, your eyelids and navel itch, you misjudge distances, you knock things over, you are clumsy as if to provide more occasions for the just-underground rages that you already feel.

"But there is one way in which men can feel exactly what it is like to experience premenstrual tension: that is to stay awake for a few nights without sleep. After this, any man is likely to experience all the symptoms....

"Some of the primitive menstrual rites appear to help the girls realize a new body-image: that which belongs to the mature woman, not the child. There is a great emphasis on the skin, its ornamentation, and the emphasizing of the body's shape by smearing with earth, plunging in water, sleeping in soft ashes, and re-clothing it. There appear opportunities for the woman to adopt as a custom some form of secluded meditation, to learn to enter deep within herself, like a descent into the underworld, or into the dream-world, during her menstrual time."

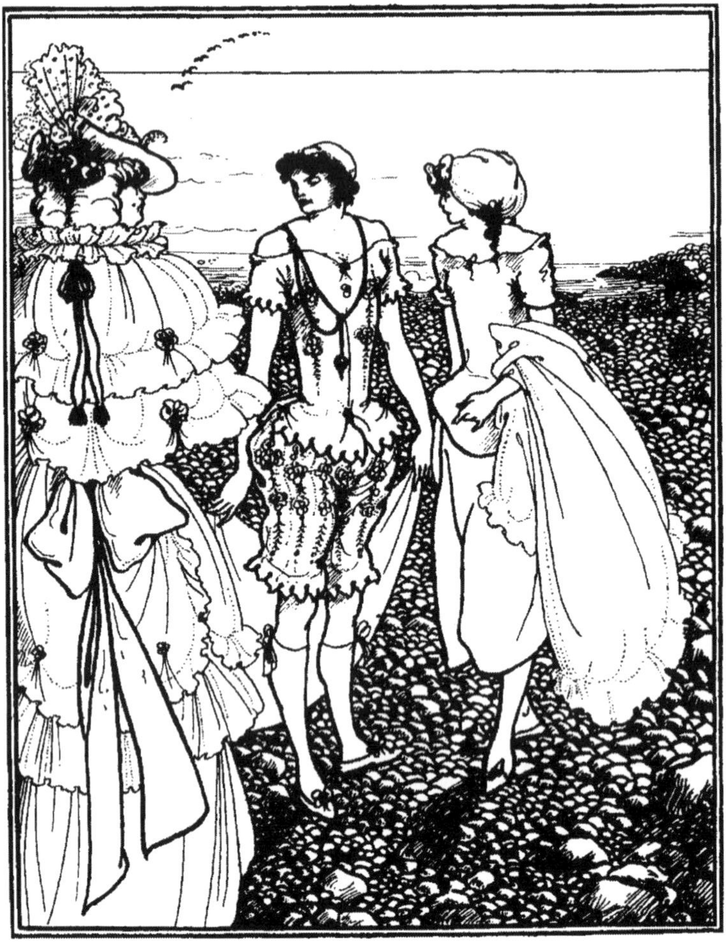

# Glow with the Flow

"The politics of PMS are as tricky as the condition," says Donna Eden. "Even women can find it hard to comprehend the impact of severe PMS. They would like it not to be true, lest it give the patriarchy an excuse to keep women from having power. What if the commander-in-chief got us into a war because of PMS! PMS has been used as evidence that women are less capable than men to be in power positions.... Women who have severe PMS symptoms are told they are 'hurting the cause' that women have been striving to achieve. It is isolating and painful to have such stigmas continue.

"I, in fact, want to go on record as saying that there is something wonderful about PMS. It insists that you move into your own rhythm rather than staying within society's time frame. Living for a few days each month from within your natural rhythm is a powerful correction to the culture's alienation from nature. PMS drops you deep into your own being, and your own truth explodes forth at this time of the month. It is a truth serum from which you cannot escape, and if you carve out a space for it, as in the native 'moon hut' traditions, PMS makes you wiser. If you do not, it can cause you to feel you are going stark raving mad. Rather than try to find a president whose hormones fit the structure of the job, why not structure the job to take advantage of someone whose hormones give them the full range of life's experiences? Policy decisions in most parts of the world could afford more compassion and family-oriented wisdom."

—Donna Eden, *Energy Medicine: Balance Your Body's Energies for Optimum Health, Joy, and Vitality*

# The Teen Scene

Clinical psychologist Dr. Mary Pipher, in *Reviving Ophelia: Saving the Selves of Adolescent Girls*, explains why, at the end of the twentieth century, girls need many years to complete the passage through puberty:

"Generally, pu-berty is defined as a biological process while adolescence is defined as the social and personal experience of that process. But even puberty is influenced by culture. Girls are menstruating much earlier now than during the colonial era, and even earlier than in the 1950s. There are many theories about why puberty comes earlier

— changes in nutrition (girls get bigger at a younger age because they are better nourished), hormones added to beef and chicken (growth hormones that are known to affect humans may trigger early puberty), and electricity (bodies are programmed to enter puberty after exposure to a certain amount of light, which comes much earlier in a woman's lifetime in an age of electricity). The point is that girls enter adolescence earlier than they did forty years ago. Some girls menstruate at age nine.

"Early puberty actually slows down many aspects of girls' development. Early development and the more difficult culture of the 1990s increase the stress on adolescents. Girls who have recently learned to bake cookies and swan-dive aren't ready to handle offers for diet pills. Girls who are reading about Pippi Longstocking aren't ready for the sexual harassment they'll encounter in schools. Girls who love to practice piano and visit their grandmothers aren't ready for the shunning by cliques. And at the same time girls must face events prematurely, they are encouraged by our culture to move away from parents and depend on friends for guidance. No wonder they suffer and make so many mistakes.

"Girls stay in adolescence longer now. In the fifties and sixties, most teens left home as soon as they graduated from high school, never to return. Increasingly in the 1980s and 1990s young adults do not want to leave home, or they leave home for a while and return to live with their parents in their twenties. Partly children stay because of economics, partly they stay because home seems a safe haven in an increasingly dangerous world. Now adolescence may begin around age ten and may last until around age twenty-two. It can take twelve years to make it through the crucible."

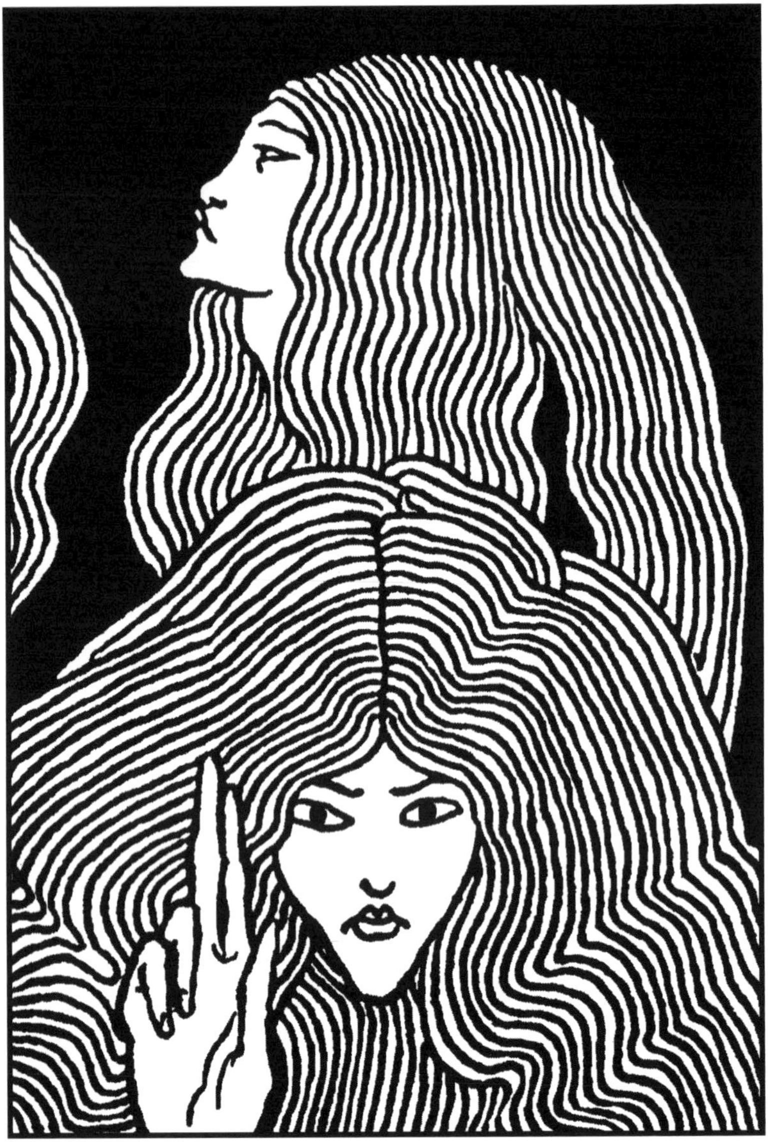

# All Together Now—1,2,3

An anthropologist named Martha McClintock published research showing that the menstrual cycles of women who are in close contact with each other will synchronize within four months. The closer the contact between the women, the closer the synchrony of their periods. This explains the menstrual synchrony in college sororities, convents, close work groups, and households with several women.

The timing of ovulation in female mammals can actually be manipulated by exposing them to stronger than normal light at different times. In fact, a woman can make her periods more regular by exposing herself during the fourteenth through sixteenth nights of her cycle to the light of a 100-watt light bulb. So now we start to understand why the menstrual cycles of women of native cultures, sleeping under the light of a full moon, couldn't help but be synchronized. Their pineal glands were all being given photic stimulation together, by the moonlight, through receptors in the skin.

# The Body Keeps Score

Dr. Christiane Northrup, a holistic obstetrician and gynecologist, is a "new breed" of doctor who synthesizes ancient wisdom with the best of modern Western medicine. In *Women's Bodies, Women's Wisdom*, she tells us how to begin our quest for health:

"Our thoughts, emotions, and brain communicate directly with our immune, nervous, and endocrine systems and with the organs of our bodies. Moreover, although these bodily systems are conventionally studied and viewed as separate, they are, in fact, aspects of the same system! If the uterus, the ovaries, the white blood cells, and the heart all make the same chemicals as the brain makes when it thinks, *where in the body is the mind?* The answer is, *The mind is located throughout the body.*

"Our entire concept of 'the mind' needs to be expanded considerably. *The mind can no longer be thought of as being confined to the brain or to the intellect; it exists in every cell of our bodies.* Every thought we think has a biochemical equivalent. Every emotion that we feel has a biochemical equivalent.... So when the part of your mind that is your uterus talks to you, through pain or excessive bleeding, are you prepared to listen to it?...

"Beliefs and memories are actually biological constructs in the body.... All living things respond physically to the way they *think* reality is.... So it is that we can be sure the events of our childhood set the stage for our beliefs about ourselves and therefore our experience, including our health. For a woman to change or improve her reality and her state of health, she first has to change her beliefs about what is possible....

"Although our entire bodies are affected by our thoughts and emotions and their various parts talk to each other, each individual's body language is unique. *No matter what has happened in her life, a woman has the power to change what that experience means to her and thus change her experience, both emotionally and physically. Therein lies her healing....*

"In order to create health daily, long before illness ensues we need to pay attention to the subtle signals from our bodies about what feels good and what doesn't. Foggy thinking, dizziness, heart palpitations, acne, headaches, and back, stomach, and pelvic pain are a few of the common but subtle symptoms that often signal that it is time for us to let go of what we don't want in life....

"Another issue for many women is shame. Shame hits the first three female centers and the associated interior organs, including the uterus and ovaries. Shame can be a result of social programming that tells a woman she's inferior,...

"Once we begin to appreciate our menstrual cycle as part of our inner guidance system, we begin to heal both hormonally and emotionally. There is no doubt that premenstrually, many women feel more inward-directed and more connected to their personal pain and the pain of the world. Many such women are also more in touch with their own creativity and get their best ideas premenstrually, though they may not act on them until later. During the premenstrual phase, we need time to be alone, time to rest, and time away from our daily duties, but taking this time is a new idea and practice for many women. Premenstrual syndrome results when we don't honor our need to ebb and flow like the tides. This society likes action, so we often don't appreciate our need for rest and replenishment. The menstrual cycle is set up to teach us about the need for both the in-breath and the out-breath of life's processes...."

# The Genius Uterus

Dr. Mona Lisa Schulz is a neuropsychiatrist and neuroscientist. In her book *Awakening Intuition*, she gives suggestions for tapping into the intuitive skills that all people possess:

"We might have a hard time believing that there's a mind in the uterus, as some physicians say, or that every part or area of the body is associated with its own specific emotions. In fact, however, scientific studies not only support such theories but clearly demonstrate that the body is the repository of actual physicalized memories of events and emotions that have befallen us and that continue to affect us in the present.

"*Memories* and their attendant emotions are stored and encoded both in our *brains* and our *bodies*. The wisdom we've gained and the traumas we've experienced are processed verbally in the brain. They're also processed nonverbally, often through stress, in the body. The brain communicates constantly with other organs, and they in turn communicate with us. The uterus, for instance, talks to you through the menstrual cycle, your stomach may communicate with you when you experience butterflies onstage, and your skin may have talked to you when you were under the stress of puberty. When intuition comes, the brain releases endorphins and neuropeptides to all the nerves, all the other organs. And a systematic organization of specific emotions and memories in the brain is being transferred to specific organs in the body. This is all part of our intuition network, our inner guidance system.

"...Studies have shown that the left brain is primed for mostly positive words such as 'joy,' 'happiness,' 'love,' and 'cheer,' while the right hemisphere picks up negative-toned words. It's been found that before ovulation, most women's abil-ity to hear words occurs chiefly in the left hemisphere, or the right ear. After ovulation, however, the right brain picks up the tempo. Now the women hear more words such as 'grief,' 'anger,' and 'depression.' This is more than an explanation for PMS. What's happening is that the brain is allowing women to hear things they don't usually want to hear. As they turn inward premenstrually, they may actually be getting more access to matters they need to hear about but ignore during the rest of their cycle. Might this be a part of intuition? You may think so after hearing this story. A friend of mine had a patient whose husband insisted that whenever she was premenstrual, she would get a sense that she should go back to school, that she needed to change her career. After her period started, she would give up these career plans and just want to serve her husband. It's not surprising that her husband had brought her in to the OB-GYN with the order to 'fix her' because she had PMS. He didn't like the intuitions she was getting about what to do with her life.

"...Women, during ovulation, frequently dream of boulders smashing through windows (eggs being released by the ovaries) or about being in a house where the walls are coming down (the uterine lining sloughing off during menstruation)....

"Scientific evidence from a fascinating study in the 1930s supports the idea that dream imagery is related to our body functions and body states. On the West Coast, a researcher would ask women to describe their dreams. On the basis of the dream content, the researcher would predict what phase of the menstrual cycle each woman was in. The doctor would figure out what the woman's ovaries and uterus were doing based solely on the content of her dreams. The women's Pap smears were then sent to a physician on the East Coast who would examine the smears and determine exactly what phase of the menstrual cycle each woman was in. In nearly every case, the prediction and the actual determination matched. Before ovulation, the women's dreams involved activities in the outer world. But during menstruation, the dreams were almost uniformly inner-directed — of staying at home, taking care of the house, nesting. The psychological content of the dreams mirrors what was going on in the woman's body."

# Thoughts R Us

Writer Caroline Myss holds the degree of Doctor of Divinity. As a medical intuitive, she worked with physicians to diagnose illnesses by intuitively reading patients' electromagnetic energy fields. In *Anatomy of the Spirit*, she makes a connection between events in our lives and illness in our bodies:

"Practitioners of energy medicine believe that the human energy field contains and reflects each individual's energy. It surrounds us and carries with us the emotional energy created by our internal and external experiences — both positive and negative. This emotional force influences the physical tissue within our bodies. In this way your biography — that is, the experiences that make up your life — becomes your biology. Experiences that carry emotional energy in our energy systems include: past and present relationships, both personal and professional; profound or traumatic experiences and memories; and belief patterns and attitudes, including all spiritual and superstitious beliefs. The emotions from these experiences become encoded in our biological systems and contribute to the formation of our cell tissue, which then generates a quality of energy that reflects those emotions.

"In a woman younger than forty, problems with menstruation, cramps, and PMS are classic indications that she is in some kind of conflict with being a woman, with her role in the tribe, and with tribal expectations of her. Most problems with bleeding and irregular periods frequently come from having too much emotional stress combined with the belief that one has no power over one's life choices, that one's choices are controlled by others. Bleeding abnormalities are often exacerbated when a woman internalizes confusing signals from her family or society about her own sexual pleasure and sexual needs."

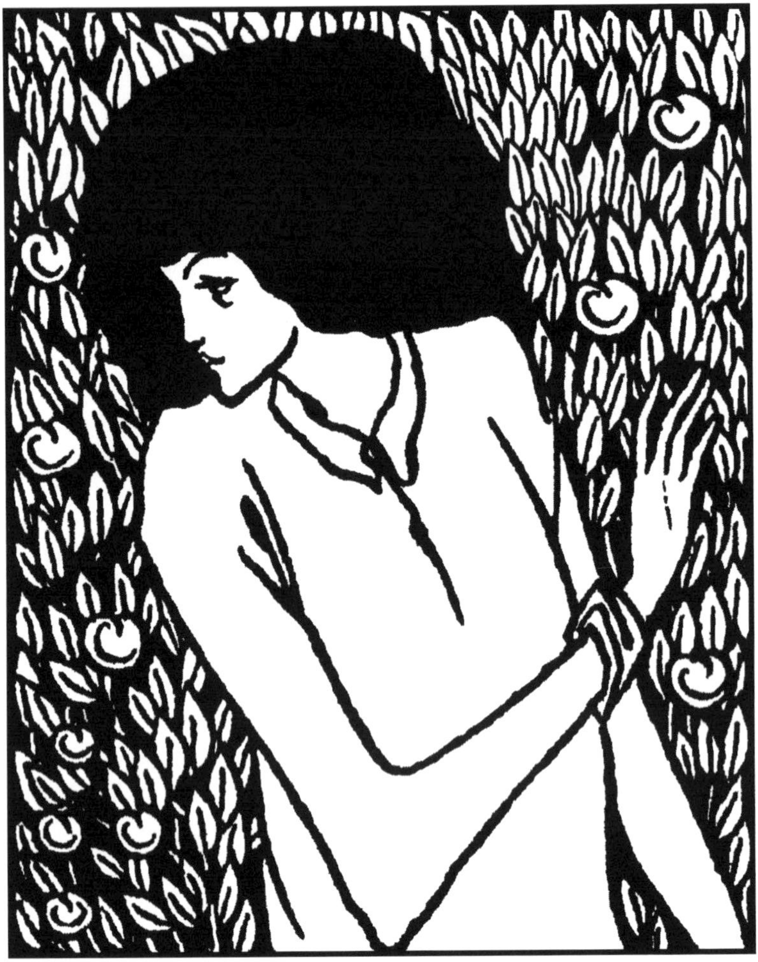

# Lady Wisdom

In *Natural Grace: Dialogues on Creation, Darkness, and the Soul in Spirituality and Science,* **Father Matthew Fox** writes of the feminine aspect of the deity in Christianity, which like the other major religions of the world, was preceded by ancient goddess cultures:

"Whenever you discover the goddess, what you're really discovering is the creative power of the community and of the individual. The goddess tradition in Christianity is the same as the Christ tradition; it's a synonym. The depths of the Mary archetype are very powerful.... There is the basic archetype of God as mother and even of Christ as mother.... This is an ancient tradition.... But the whole idea is balance.... If we live in a religious era that does not honor the motherhood of God and the Goddess along with the fatherhood of God, then we have impoverished souls....

"So a time for recovering the goddess tradition essentially teaches that the creative energies of the Universe and the maker of the Universe are in all things. It's a moment of celebration of creativity. As we know, in that five-thousand-year period in Europe when they worshiped the mother goddess, we have found no evidence of any military artifacts. Instead, what we have found are tens of thousands of statuettes of pregnant women...."

# Ancient Future

"It has been suggested that movement and preparation of the female egg for possible fertilization is a recapitulation of the coming into being of the earth and of humanity, that stored within a woman's monthly cycle is an ancient memory of the evolution of spirit into matter. To find our way to this memory of cosmic origins is our task as women preparing for the future within the vessel of our body as temple, our cycle as sacrament, with the sacred on a mission of love."

— Tamara Slayton, founder, Menstrual Health Foundation

# Remember When God Was a Woman

And now we come full circle, with greater understanding,
to the words from a pagan chant:

Warm caress in the nighttime,
Tender lip of the rose at dawn,
Echoing crypt in the shadows,
Can you tell me where she's gone?

Do you remember when god was a woman?
She had many, many names;
We called her Isis, Astarte, Diana,
Hecate, Demeter, Kali, Inanna.

She was mother and all her children
In the skies and the lands and the seas;
She was the ripening green one,
Giving life abundantly.

She was waxing moon and its waning,
Sun and stars, queen of heaven too;
She was deep space and the galaxies
That we ride twirling through.

We heard her voice in the whirlwind;
Sensed her pulse in the tide of the seas.
We tasted her flesh in the growing rain,
Felt her blood giving birth painfully.

*Ebb and Flow*

She was the young maiden huntress,
New life that bloomed in the spring;
She was the seed of beginning,
The door that was opening.

She was the crone, hag of wisdom,
The deep grave under the earth;
She was mistress of night and darkness,
Face of death and cauldron of rebirth.

She was the caress in the nighttime
And tender lip of the rose at dawn,
She was the echo in the shadows.
Can you tell me where she's gone?

She is the lover, sweet passion's desire,
Healing man and woman too.
She's the skin and mouth, the swelling breast,
The gate we all pass through.

She's the world outside and inside;
She is near and center and far.
She is north and south, east and west;
She's the tail of the shooting star.

She's the woman crying for justice,
The pain still locked in her womb.
She moves in the power of changing,
And she calls for ancient freedom.

Do you remember when god
   was a woman?
She had many, many names.
Do you remember when god
   was a woman?
She had many, many names
         —Author Unknown

Grateful acknowledgment is given for permission to reprint from the following:

From *Awakening Intuition* by Mona Lisa Schulz. Copyright © 1998 by Mona Lisa Schulz. Reprinted by permission of Harmony Books, a division of Random House, Inc.

From *Reviving Ophelia* by Mary Pipher, Ph.D. Copyright © 1994 by Mary Pipher, Ph.D. Used by permission of Putnam Berkley, a division of Penguin Putnam Inc.

From *The Red Tent* by Anita Diamant. Copyright © 1997 by Anita Diamant. Reprinted by permission of St. Martin's Press, LLC.

From *Women's Bodies, Women's Wisdom* by Christiane Northrup, M.D. Copyright © 1994, 1998 by Christiane Northrup, M.D. Used by permission of Bantam Books, a division of Random House, Inc.

**What's *your* story?**
If you have an indelible memory of being tortured by (or making peace with) your uterus that you would like to share for *Tales of the Curse II*, please email it to the "Contact Us" page of www.lumpkinweb.com. Thanks!

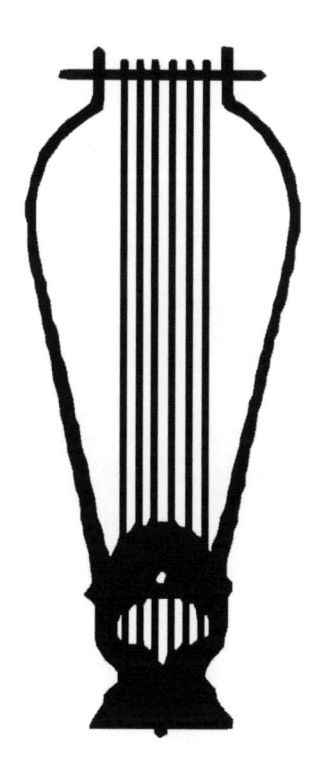

Made in the USA